TRANSFORMATIVE INNOVATION

A GUIDE TO PRACTICE AND POLICY

Graham Leicester

First published in 2016
Second edition: 2016

Published by:

Triarchy Press

Axminster, England

info@triarchypress.net ~ www.triarchypress.net

with International Futures Forum

Aberdour, Scotland

www.internationalfuturesforum.com ~ www.iffpraxis.com

A catalogue record for this book is available from the British Library.

Print ISBN: 978-1-911193-00-5
ePub ISBN: 978-1-911193-01-2

Artwork by Jennifer Williams. Jennifer Williams is critically acclaimed at making hand-made books, cut-outs, photographs, illustrations, prints and puppets. She is a trustee and member of International Futures Forum and for 31 years directed the Centre for Creative Communities.

This book could not have been written without the remarkable learning community that is IFF. Each of its members has held their own considerable knowledge lightly in a generous collective pursuit over many years of fresh insight available only to those willing to wrestle with fundamental themes and challenge the safe bet of conventional wisdom in service of the greater good.

CONTENTS

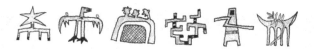

The Practice of Transformative Innovation

In December 2000 an invitation was issued to around thirty leading figures from different disciplines and different parts of the world to join International Futures Forum, a two-year project to discover how to take more effective action in a complex world we don't understand and cannot control. They were invited:

> *...to explore the nature of the most significant future challenges facing society and the systemic connections between them; to examine ways in which we might successfully adapt and respond to these challenges, including by learning from existing promising practice; and to stimulate actions consonant with that inquiry by individual communities and at a systemic level, in Scotland and elsewhere.*

That two-year project has prompted a further decade and more of international inquiry. It has furnished an extensive and still growing body of new theory and critical thinking.

Yet the central mission has always been to support effectiveness in action. IFF has diligently worked in diverse settings, with government, business and in local community settings, to test and elaborate our emerging understandings in practice.

We learned early on that effective action in today's complex world requires three essential orientations:

- take the broadest possible view of the context, always thinking systemically, combining holism with focus.

- think in terms of long-term transitions: what brought today's challenges into being, and how might things develop in the future? The late California Senator John Vasconcellos told us that the task is to be hospice workers for the dying culture and midwives for the new.

- always remember that whatever else is in play we will be dealing with a human system. As the great systems theorist Sir Geoffrey Vickers observed: human systems are different.

These orientations only get us so far. There is still the question of what we should actually _do._ If at some level we feel our current actions are _ineffective_, then the answer is apparently simple. We must change. We must try something different. We must innovate.

But what kind of innovation? I well recall a conversation with the distillery manager at Lagavulin on Islay, producer of one of the finest single malt whiskies in the world. He told me he was moving on after five years in post. "I'm starting to run out of ideas for how to keep the product the same", he told me, unconsciously echoing the words of Lampedusa ("If we want things to stay the same, everything must change").

Maintaining our existing systems against the grain of a changing world requires constant innovation – making things faster, cheaper, smarter, safer or substituting for elements which have become scarce those that are more abundant.

These are necessary aims. But for those with an eye on the unfolding future they are not sufficient. If we sense that the existing system is fundamentally unsustainable in the longer term, then a different kind of innovation is needed. We must redesign the plane even whilst doing our damnedest to keep it in the air.

The redesign involves directing creative effort towards growing a viable system for the future rather than simply making the best of the one we have. It requires us to build organisation and infrastructure for the new system as it grows. And it invites us to draw on an innate human capacity to act in tune with and realise our deeper aspirations in a complex world rather than just settle for fixing what's failing. This last, it turns out, is the key to *really* effective action, not just for policy or organisations but also at a personal level.

This is the practice of 'transformative innovation'.

The Capacity to Innovate

Perhaps we can all point to some initiatives that have this quality. We may even be fortunate enough to be involved in some. But transformative innovation is rare at scale. It is usually seen as counter-cultural by dominant business-as-usual systems. They therefore tend either to suppress it or absorb it – the latter usually being called 'scaling' or 'mainstreaming'. So the fate of most promising innovations with the potential to transform is either to run out of steam and end up as shining, one-off, small-scale examples, or to be absorbed into the dominant system to improve its efficiency and prolong its life.

Neither outcome fulfils the innovation's transformative potential. Both feel like failure and disappointment to the initiators: their aspirational vision remains no nearer realisation and long-term, systemic challenges seem as intractable as ever.

Alongside the practice therefore, we clearly need to get smarter about the systems and structures that support transformative innovation and realise its potential. This is particularly true in the social and public spheres where there is no equivalent of the natural dynamics of the market to drive waves of innovation and 'creative destruction'.

Market innovation systems, after all, have become highly sophisticated. Each phase has distinct institutions and financing mechanisms. There are research funds, prize awards, 'google time' and so on for speculative idea generation at the pioneering stage. Then venture capital, alternative investment markets and business incubators for start-ups. Finally, the stock market, pension funds, the investment banks and the big chains exist to service the needs of the mass market.

Compare this with the non-commercial sectors engaged in the pursuit of civic goods and social change – the public, social, civic and philanthropic sectors for whom this book is written. There is no shortage of creative ideas and radical intent in our public and social agencies. Many develop into impressive projects, detailed in encouraging reports and conference platform presentations. Yet still these examples remain the exception, and the wider systems and culture in which they are introduced carry on their course untroubled. They are like seeds falling on stony ground: some occasionally germinate, but even they are unlikely to reach their full potential.

If we are to get better at this and allow our radical seedlings to grow into sturdy new plants that themselves configure whole new habitats, then we need to learn from the commercial world: we must understand how patterns of renewal function in social and policy systems beyond the market and put in place the infrastructure to support them. In other words, we need *both* to nurture an intentional practice of transformative innovation *and* put dedicated systems in place to support it.

The practice therefore requires:

- Individuals and team leaders working in the public and social sectors who can see that existing patterns of activity are unsustainable and want to discover and put into practice a better way.

- Leaders of organisations, policy- and strategy-makers, who understand how to support and foster transformative innovation as a practice distinct from sustaining or disruptive innovation.

- Finance specialists who can design systems to handle the resource implications of transformative innovation, both to feed initiatives at the critical points where they need support (they require very little finance to get started) and to plan for the long-term transfer of sunk costs from our failing systems into new patterns ready to support the load.

This book addresses all three features in six chapters that echo to some extent the central requirements of 'education for the 21st century' published by Jacques Delors' UNESCO Commission in 1996 – learning to know, learning to be, learning to do and learning to live, together. This reference points to the fact that the practice of transformative innovation is fundamentally about a development of the capacities of the individuals, teams and institutions involved.

The six chapters are:

- *Knowing:* the first challenge is to shift our ways of making sense of the operating environment so that we become comfortable with its complexity rather than overwhelmed by it. This is the substance of Chapter 2.

- *Imagining:* the next challenge is to respond to the question that will inevitably have arisen from our contemplation of the contemporary world – what is to be done? What is the transformative innovation that needs to be embodied and initiated? There are countless possibilities. What are the processes that will help guide us towards a 'wise initiative' – one with the best chance of success in the real world whilst also carrying the hopes and aspirations of the initiating group? This is covered in Chapter 3.

- *Being:* the next challenge is to bring a group of people together to take this step, to move outside the comfort of simply improving what is in place and to make a stand for something radically different. The group needs to be organised, led and managed to succeed. It needs to expand over time. And its members, particularly the pioneers, must not burn out. This is the subject of Chapter 4.

- *Doing:* the test is effectiveness in action, over time. Chapter 5 shows how to introduce the new in the presence of the old and gradually grow it as a process of reflective learning. It introduces specific tools for dealing with challenges likely to be encountered along the way: enrolling others, taking difficult decisions, figuring out what to do when you don't know what to do.

- *Enabling:* most of this guide is directed at the innovators, the intrepid souls ready to try to shift the system from an unsustainable business-as-usual approach towards a new pattern of viability. But their task is made much easier if the conditions are in place to enable rather than hamper the transition. Chapter 6 considers how policy, strategy and, in particular, finance can enable more transformative innovation.

- *Supporting:* beyond policy and finance, the final chapter describes and makes the case for investing in intentionally designed *systems and structures* to support a culture of renewal in our public, civic and social systems in just the way that market-based systems and structures have evolved to support commercial innovation. IFF has begun to put in place a dedicated infrastructure to support transformative innovation – to demonstrate what is possible and to encourage others to follow suit.

Practice and Theory

The book is designed as a *practical* guide, not a theoretical treatise. It distils the generic learning from years of practice. In order to keep it short there is scant reference to specific examples in the text. Instead each chapter, including this one, concludes with suggestions for further reading – including pamphlets and resources that can be freely downloaded from the IFF Practice Centre at www.iffpraxis.com/ti.

There are no footnotes. The book draws for its theoretical underpinning principally on the work of core IFF members over many years of collaborative inquiry. It could not have been written without them. They are named throughout and there is a full list of members included as an appendix. Where other sources are cited there is always enough information in the text to allow you to track them down.

The intention is that this guide, supplemented where necessary by the additional materials listed at the end of each chapter, will be all you need to initiate or support transformative innovation in your own sphere. If you feel the need for a concrete example as you read, then turn to the case study of the SHINE programme in Fife.

SHINE: Changing the Culture of Care tells the story of a new approach to older people's care in one region of Scotland – an initiative that IFF has supported from its early imaginings in 2009. The programme has followed the innovator's dream of a ten-fold increase in coverage every year and has begun to attract national attention – most recently as an example of best practice included in a Health Foundation and Nesta report, *At The Heart of Health: realising the value of people and communities.*

What the existing reports on SHINE miss, however, is that it has been a rare example of transformative innovation that has started to realise its potential at scale. It has been driven from within the system rather than from above or from outside, could easily have been written off as an abject failure at any time in its first two years, has been based on a change in practice by existing staff rather than the investment of significant new resource, and would not have happened without the persistent, dedicated and artful commitment of a small group of pioneers.

The full case study is published separately and referenced at the end of the chapter, but there is a brief summary of the SHINE story (starting on page 21) to whet your appetite and to serve as a point of reference in practice for the chapters that follow.

Those chapters naturally occur in a certain order. But they do not have to be read that way. Certainly they do not need to be applied in that way. In the real world, transformative innovation is a complex, messy, creative process. This is not a textbook for diligent, step-by-step study. Rather, it is a book for dipping into as a source of encouragement, reassurance, guidance, confirmation, insight, suggestion and refreshment. My hope is that you might open it at any page and find something there that will help evoke the hidden resources to take your work forward. That's what the world needs.

Ten Characteristics of Transformative Innovation

By way of orientation for the chapters that follow, it will be helpful first to spend a little more time on the distinguishing characteristics of transformative innovation and what it looks and feels like in practice.

The concept is most easily understood with reference to the Three Horizons framework, which IFF has used extensively both to help individuals, groups and organisations understand the need to break free from the constraints of 'business as usual' and provide a framework to translate that aspiration into effective action.

The framework (which is discussed in more detail in Chapter 3) sees a mainstream 'first horizon' system losing effectiveness and therefore dominance over time (the red line); a 'second horizon' of innovations seeking to exploit opportunities emerging in the changing world (the blue line); and a 'third horizon' in tune with deeper trends and changes that eventually emerges as the new dominant pattern – perhaps a generation from now (the green line).

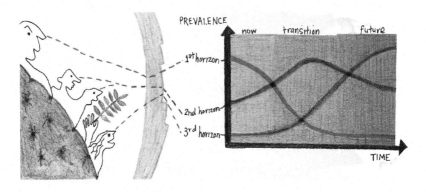

TRANSFORMATIVE INNOVATION

Some innovations will ease the pathway towards the third horizon. Others will be taken up by the first horizon system to extend its life a little longer. The distinction recalls Clayton Christensen's description of the difference between '*sustaining innovation*', which improves the efficiency and prolongs the life of existing systems, and '*disruptive innovation*', which disrupts or subverts those systems.

The Three Horizons model shows that if we take a longer view there is also a third form of innovation – *transformative innovation* – which intentionally shifts existing systems towards a new pattern of activity suited to the changed environment. Anyone can disrupt a system. But you need a third horizon to disrupt it with a purpose.

In the course of our work we have identified ten critical characteristics of such innovation. It is:

1. *Balanced: paying skilful attention to the twin requirements to be hospice workers for the dying culture and midwives for the new, consciously operating in both worlds at the same time.* This is the critical skillset, mastering the skills of tact, timing and titration (choosing the right dose, not pushing our luck) that allow us to keep the old culture on board even as we introduce radical innovation designed to transition to a new pattern.

2. *Inspiring and hopeful for the participants and for others who come to know or hear about it.* It has this quality because it effectively acknowledges the broader cultural unease with 'business as usual' and is not just another 'patch' on the system.

3. *Informed by a longer-term perspective, taking the future into account.* We cannot be midwives to better future outcomes without this perspective.

4. *Pioneering: trying something new and counter-cultural, starting small, rooted in discovery and learning – rather than the application of tried and tested procedures.* If we are going to shift the culture then we must do something that will be seen as 'counter-cultural' in today's terms. And if so, we should start small: anything bigger can be seen as too threatening or resource-intensive and may be suppressed.

5. *Grounded: facing up to reality, generated from a clear-sighted view of the evidence but not hidebound by it, taking knowledge gained from lived experience as seriously as abstract data.* The transformative initiative will be based on a long-term aspiration, but must take its place in the messy reality of the present. We ignore that at our peril.

6. *Based on personal commitment 'beyond reason', with the individuals involved stepping out of their formal roles and into themselves.* This means bringing our full selves to the challenge, giving us access to capacities, resources and stories we usually keep in the background in our professional lives — our own passions and aspirations, for example. We will need all of this to carry out transformative innovation successfully.

7. *Responsible: honouring the principle of 'first do no harm', sensitive to the pressures on people pushing the boundaries and not pushing too far too fast.* While this kind of work is invigorating and fulfilling, it will also demand a lot from us. It can start to ask too much. We must look after ourselves and each other. The catalyst will have failed if it burns up in the experiment.

8. *Revealing hidden resources – by freeing up resources locked into the existing system and by configuring new sources of abundance.* It is scarcity that is undermining the effectiveness of our present systems. The trajectory of transformative innovation needs to be towards sources of support that are abundant and away from reliance on those that are scarce. This kind of work is attractive – people will want to get involved. Hidden resources will emerge.

9. *Maintaining integrity, coherence, wholeness at all scales and from all perspectives, with words and deeds, being and doing in alignment.* Every action carries an implicit culture with it that can and will be inferred both from what is done and how it is pursued. Authenticity is vital, and attractive. It is not that the means determine the ends. The means are the ends.

10. *Maintaining a pioneering spirit even in the face of success, preferring to be followed by, rather than swallowed by, the mainstream system.* It can be very difficult to resist siren calls to 'mainstream' any innovation that does well. The overwhelming instinct of a system in decline is to search around for innovations that will save it. But propping up the old system will not hasten the arrival of the new – and may make its eventual appearance all the more costly and painful. The ultimate aim here is to transform the culture, to free up resources sunk into maintaining today's system so that they can be rechannelled towards a system that is fit for tomorrow.

Case Study: SHINE ~ Changing the Culture of Care

Overview

The SHINE programme was initiated in spring 2011 by NHS Fife and partners Fife Council, Community Catalysts, BRAG Enterprises and International Futures Forum with one year's funding from a Health Foundation 'invest to save' grant.

It introduced a new way of helping older people to 'not only survive but thrive' at home by asking not 'what is the matter with you?' and then checking for eligibility for standard services, but instead 'what matters to you?' and then configuring resources, including those of friends, family, neighbours and the local community, around the answer.

The intention was to introduce a person-centred, relational practice: to mobilise the individual's own inner resources and their motivation to restore or maintain their desired pattern of life. The programme also envisaged establishing a range of local 'microproviders' to cater to the variety of personalised and bespoke needs revealed in the process.

Imagining

The origins of the programme can be traced to a Three Horizons conversation in 2009 on winter planning for NHS Fife. Every winter the hospitals fill up, including with older people whose living circumstances then come under scrutiny and whose discharge from hospital is often delayed while suitable care at home is put in place.

The conversation revealed a third horizon vision of a very different, all-pervasive culture of care. The love and fear loops (see page 39) provided a simple graphic reminder of the shift in culture required.

The Nuka system of care in Alaska was identified as a living example of this third horizon vision. A series of exchange visits followed between Fife and Alaska which have since contributed to introducing Nuka widely in the UK.

Helping older people to thrive at home was identified as a first step on the journey to the third horizon for NHS Fife. A small group formed a committed integrity to pursue this initiative (see page 61), which was understood as a series of iterations of a social learning cycle (see page 72).

In 2010 the Health Foundation opened a grant programme called SHINE. It invited 'invest to save' proposals which could deliver significant savings in healthcare spending within a year. The Fife team successfully bid for one year's funding, but suggested that the savings from their programme would only come after two years – when they anticipated the closure of a continuing care ward in a community hospital. What became known as the SHINE programme in Fife got under way in spring 2011.

At the end of each year of the programme IFF has hosted a day of learning and reflection. The notes that follow provide the headlines from each year in a common format. Those on the 'First Horizon Context' describe changes in dominant first horizon systems and the overall operating environment.

Year One ============

Results: 6 older people experience the new approach.

First Horizon Context: SHINE fits well into existing policy frameworks: health and social care integration, reshaping care for older people, the move to 'coproduction' and 'assets-based' approaches. But in practice first horizon structures are preoccupied with the challenges of reorganisation and budget cuts.

Reflections: The project bid promised 30 patients would experience the new approach by the end of year one. There have been only six. It promised sufficient coverage to close a continuing care ward at the end of year two. The ward has been closed anyway. It is proving difficult to open up this kind of honest and personal conversation with older people. The need to record data and to get official consent to be part of the experimental programme makes it even more difficult. The programme tried to spread too far too fast: introducing this new approach successfully requires an intensity of effort. The personal shift in practice can be painful – tears flow. But the stories told by the patients who have participated are heart-warming and humbling. This is not about the money. A little hope goes a long way.

Year Two ============

Results: 50 older people experience the new approach.

First Horizon Context: The Health Foundation offers new funding to appoint 'Clinical Champions' to help spread the new practice. The principal funder – essentially covering a part-time producer role (see page 65) – is now the Scottish Government's Joint Improvement Team with additional resources from their 'Change Fund'. This brings with it a new set of measures and accountabilities but no clear strategic coherence. The referendum on independence starts to dominate the political context. Microproviders in particular start to encounter regulations and 'red tape' in a regulatory system that never anticipated organisations operating at this small scale.

Reflections: The project bid promised 100 people involved by this point. There are only 50. But this is a slow, organic process: skyscrapers go up overnight while trees take time to grow. There is a dawning realisation that the conversation about 'personal outcomes' is an intervention in itself and boosts the capacity of the patient. BRAG – the social enterprise hub responsible for incubating the microproviders – offers tea parties for local older people and as a result starts to provide facilities for new community activities. Measurement of outcomes seems inevitably to be conducted on first horizon terms, particularly economic benefit. Yet an evaluation of the programme so far describes the change in practice as 'subtle but profound'. Peer support for staff changing their practice is found to be a critical ingredient – this is not just about picking up a new method, it is a personal shift.

SHINE: Changing the Culture of Care

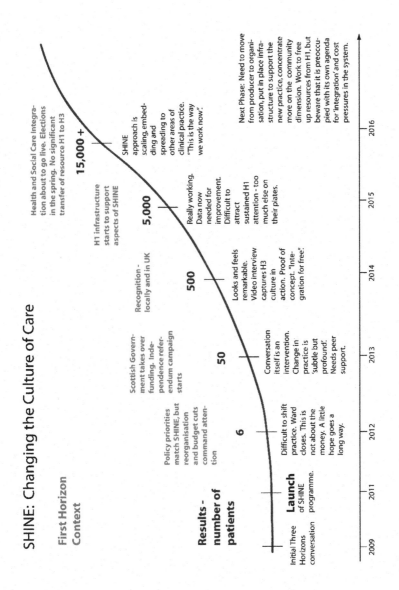

First Horizon Context

Initial Three Horizons conversation

Policy priorities match SHINE, but reorganisation and budget cuts command attention

Scottish Government takes over funding. Independence referendum campaign starts

Recognition - locally and in UK

H1 infrastructure starts to support aspects of SHINE

Health and Social Care Integration about to go live. Elections in the spring. No significant transfer of resource H1 to H3

SHINE approach is scaling, embedding and spreading to other areas of clinical practice. "This is the way we work now."

Next Phase: Need to move from producer to organisation, put in place infrastructure to support the new practice, concentrate more on the community dimension. Work to free up resources from H1, but beware that it is preoccupied with its own agenda for 'integration' and cost pressures in the system.

Results - number of patients

Launch of SHINE programme.

6

50

500

5,000

15,000 +

Difficult to shift practice. Ward closes. This is not about the money. A little hope goes a long way.

Conversation itself is an intervention. Change in practice is 'subtle but profound'. Needs peer support.

Looks and feels remarkable. Video interview captures H3 culture in action. Proof of concept. "Integration for free."

Really working. Data now needed for improvement. Difficult to attract sustained H1 attention - too much else on their plates.

2009   2011   2012   2013   2014   2015   2016

TRANSFORMATIVE INNOVATION

Year Three ============

Results: 500 people now experiencing the new approach.

First Horizon Context: Recognition. SHINE is beginning to attract attention in Scotland and more widely across the UK. Everyone is talking about personal outcomes; Fife is actually doing it.

Reflections: The project begins to look and feel significant. It is light on measures and evidence of economic impact – not for want of trying. It is difficult to gather data from frail older people and to measure 'results on the inside'. Patient stories are remarkable. One in particular, which has been captured on video, is powerfully moving and epitomises the new culture of care envisioned in 2009. Some first horizon support (including a little money) is materialising – with the explicit warning that it comes with a 'black belt in stifling the life out of organic initiatives'. In the overall policy context of health and social care integration, it is clear that the SHINE approach, configuring resources around the aspirations of the patient, delivers "integration for free".

Year Four ============

Results: 5,000 people now experiencing the new approach. This is a conservative estimate based on sampling across Fife.

First Horizon Context: An existing 'Good Conversations' training package proves just right for introducing staff to the 'personal outcomes conversation' as a change of practice. Asset mapping begins in local communities as part of a wider ABCD (asset based community development) programme: the microprovider work can dovetail with this. Electronic systems in Fife are now adapted to take the notes/

records from the new practice. Still no first horizon institutional authority is ready to stand behind the 'Quality Mark' for microproviders.

Reflections: Everything is going well in the programme, except for engagement with senior managers and the quest to free up first horizon resources. The first horizon is under too much pressure. "You can set up a meeting with five senior managers months ahead of time, keep checking right up until the day, and in the event three of them will have to cry off – called away to other urgent business, off sick, dealing with family challenges, called in to see government officials and so on". In these circumstances we will just have to grow our own infrastructure. The data is now needed not to prove the new approach works but to manage and improve its performance. Social work – who have been working on the parallel introduction of 'self-directed support' – are now fully on board: "I feel like I belong".

Year Five ==============

Results: Difficult to estimate. 200 people have undertaken 'Good Conversations' training and their caseload must be in excess of 15,000 people experiencing the new approach. SHINE is spreading beyond older people – to podiatry, musculoskeletal clinics, stroke units and so on. So it is more difficult than ever to keep track of coverage.

First Horizon Context: Health and Social Care Integration (marriage of local council and NHS) about to go live. Senior management preoccupied with that. Many local structures in flux or dismantled. Scottish elections in the spring. Further cost pressures anticipated. Concerns that SHINE may get caught in the crossfire and that integration may bring in a new set of indicators that do not do justice to the SHINE programme. Still no sign of resource transfer from first to third horizons: finding the budget to keep the part-time producer on will be a challenge as in all previous years.

Reflections: Overall the story is one of *scaling* (increasing the numbers of people involved), *embedding* (making this approach 'the way things are done around here') and *spreading* (introducing the approach in other areas). Each new area adopts the approach in its own way. The embedding is subtle – there are changes in language in the workplace, and there is change in recruitment and induction processes.

Relationships are key to spreading, scaling and embedding. Joint training helps to establish relationships naturally. The quality of the personal outcomes conversations with patients is improving. They are aspiring for more – the patients' own sense of possibility is expanding, and there are now more options to work with their aspirations once expressed.

Patient stories remain inspirational. And records now on the electronic system mean real-time 'run charts' of data are available. Doggedness is identified as a key enabler for getting this new approach embedded: 'we don't give up'. There are some worries that key personnel are retiring or leaving for other roles: need to consolidate the infrastructure to support the new approach. That includes moving from a single part-time producer to a more robust organisation. But beware the danger of being 'captured' by the first horizon if we 'borrow' their infrastructure. There has still been no really robust evaluation in spite of best efforts. It needs time and money: both of these are in short supply. This really requires an external view.

Next Phase

The reflection day at the end of year five revealed that different parts of the system, and different individuals, are at different stages of the journey towards the third horizon aspiration. Some are just starting out with the new practice, others have been with it from the start – and are beginning to move on to other roles. Hence the primary concern to design a minimal working infrastructure, inside the wider system, to support the SHINE approach. Mirroring the producer competencies now supplied by an individual in an organisation would be a good next step (see page 65).

The community resource aspect of the approach has also taken a back seat to the change in practice by health professionals. It has been a tougher challenge. There has been no equivalent to the 'Good Conversations' training to support a shift in practice (only in Fife does this training include reference to community resource and microproviders). The money for BRAG Enterprises (the incubator for microproviders) ran out two years ago and now the Director involved from the start is moving on. It may be time to treat the community microprovider element of the SHINE approach as a new 'transformative innovation' in its own right in order to grow local capacity. A local currency may start a wider and richer local conversation, out of which a new creative integrity might emerge. Finally, other areas of Scotland are now interested in adopting their own version of the SHINE approach.

What Helped?

Interviews with the core team involved in the SHINE programme reveal a number of factors that have helped them succeed:

- Configure around commitment (IFF call this forming an 'integrity').

- See the whole programme as an intentional shift in culture, including in how we think (thinking prompts, IFF challenge to expand ways of knowing, etc.).

- Conceptual coherence: it helps to have 'maps for the journey', including the Three Horizons map and the social learning cycle.

- Producer skills, not just project management.

- Support for each other – human, open and honest.

Further Reading – details at www.iffpraxis.com/ti

SHINE: Changing the Culture of Care

Complexity Is Your Friend

When we first embarked on our inquiry into how to take more effective action in a world we don't understand and cannot control, IFF took as its starting point the assumptions, values and principles that underpin the worldview that is Enlightenment rationalism. How might these need to be extended or reimagined in order for us to gain a better grasp on the contemporary world?

Our focus was partly on the growing number of challenges, local and global, that were seemingly insoluble with the kind of thinking that had created them. It seemed to us even then that we were living in a new, networked economy in which the old rules were being subverted. The political institutions bequeathed to us by the 18th century were suffering a twin crisis of legitimacy and competence. Adam Smith's idea of the 'invisible hand' – suggesting that economic self-interest will eventually benefit society as a whole – had allowed a combination of threats to our ecosystem to accumulate that were now endangering our survival. And the triumph of reason and of modern science was leaving us alienated from the life of the spirit, searching for meaning.

Our initial inquiry therefore concentrated on the 'conceptual emergency' that seemed to underlie many of our contemporary problems: the fact that the concepts we rely on to make sense of the world no longer enable us to act effectively in it.

Adam Kahane has described a contemporary world that is complex in three distinct ways: *dynamic complexity* refers to the distance in time and space between cause and effect; *generative complexity* refers to the openness of the future and situations where the future cannot be predicted from the patterns of the past; and *social complexity* refers to the variety of actors likely to be involved, the worldviews and perspectives they are likely to bring and the complexity of relationships amongst and between them.

In most cases now when we seek to act on an issue that is important to us we are facing all three kinds of complexity simultaneously. Bob Horn talks of 'social messes' – which are combinations of problems that are systemically interlinked *plus other messes.*

In the face of such complexity it is very easy to become overwhelmed. At a psychological level there are both personal and societal consequences – which I will pick up on in the next chapter. Harvard psychologist Robert Kegan, in *In Over Our Heads: the mental demands of modern life,* points to this sense of overwhelm as in part a result of being trapped in ways of knowing (consciousness) that simply don't have the requisite variety to cope with the complexities of the contemporary world.

We need to expand our worldview, draw on more of our innate capacities for making sense and meaning, in order to restore our capacity for effective action – and effective living. That will reduce the fear and anxiety induced by not understanding, and the sense of overwhelm that boundless connectivity, information overload and rapid change can trigger.

In short, we need to make complexity our friend. Life proceeds through the development of ever more complex organisms, generating unlimited variety and diversity. We don't complain about that. Quite the contrary, we see it as enhancing the beauty we find in the world. Just so, our own lives become more complex as we develop, enveloping us in a web of knowledge, relationships, connections, memories and so on. Again, we look on this as a source of richness and development, not something to fear. As the philosopher Alfred North Whitehead said, life, the process of 'becoming', is "a creative advance into novelty".

This approach to knowing and being is a prerequisite for effective action in a complex world. As Whitehead suggests, it should come to us as easily as life itself. But this natural disposition is overlaid with centuries of privileging other kinds of intelligence. We need guidance on how to bring our wider capacities into play.

What follows is a selection:

- *Five principles:* five shifts we can make to extend our worldview beyond Enlightenment rationalism to embrace more of what we are and what we know.

- *Two loops:* reminding us that there are two fundamental ways of knowing the world and that with this awareness we can more readily move deliberately between them.

- *A variety of prompts:* simple pointers to help adjust our default modes of thinking and nudge us into a consciousness that embraces complexity as our friend.

Five Principles

1.   *From Subject-Object to Subject-Subject*

Many of the triumphs of Enlightenment rationalist thinking came from taking the objective viewpoint, separating the observer from the thing observed. That is a partial view. It needs to be complemented by a shift in our worldview that enables us to see ourselves as subjects and participants – a relational universe.

This relates to Carl Rogers' concept of the 'person' rather than the 'individual'. A person exists only in relationship, living a life in a pattern of other lives. There are likewise 'mutual' qualities of life, which cannot be fully realised by an individual but only through shared patterns of life. Language is one such quality; health is another: you cannot be healthy alone.

The triumphs of Enlightenment reason came from suppressing this subject-subject worldview. Think of it as the difference between phoning home to say you are stuck in traffic and phoning to say that you *are* traffic.

2. *Expand What Constitutes Valid Knowledge*

We tend to honour and privilege a small subset of human knowledge based on abstract rationalism. In a complex world we need to expand our worldview to include 'non-rational' knowledge as found in the arts, music, intuition, acts of the imagination, embodied knowledge, the science of qualities as much as in the science of quantities.

We also need to value collective knowledge that emerges in groups, knowledge that arises out of being in relationship (no one is as intelligent as everyone). Likewise, knowledge that rests in communities, indigenous knowledge. All knowledge is local, contextual, the product of a culture.

In the West we have elevated some forms of knowing over others – see the syllabus at our elite universities. A more equal politics of knowing will admit the broader range of knowledge we will need to make effective decisions. Max Boisot suggests that a decision is only as wise as the breadth of context we have taken into account in reaching it.

In Enlightenment thinking, the gold standard for what counts as knowledge is 'justified, true belief'. This shift requires us to open the door to knowledge that we believe and that is true of the world, but cannot (yet, or by conventional means) be justified.

3. From Organisation to Integrity

The shift from organisation to integrity is discussed in detail in the book I wrote with Maureen O'Hara *Dancing at the Edge: competence, culture and organisation in the 21st century*. It is inspired by the work of Martin Albrow and his observation that the classic model of an organisation getting aligned to impose its will on the world no longer applies.

Rather, any 'organisation' is now a dynamic pattern of relationships between its own members and between them and an ever-changing world of competing loyalties and different value systems. It is a human system, a 'human being'. Albrow calls this an 'integrity' – an organisational form that maintains a moral purpose over time. Individuals will belong to many different integrities: organisations, political parties, social clubs, the family and so on. Each negotiates its relationship with the world around the four dimensions of sovereignty, reciprocity, recognition and agency – described in more detail in discussion of the Integrity model in Chapter 4.

This model has proven a great diagnostic for groups and teams. If there is a weakness or deficit in any of these four dimensions, look at the state of the others. It is also possible to pay attention to these four dimensions intentionally to form an integrity. This is particularly useful in pursuing transformative innovation – and will be covered in more detail in the chapter on 'being'.

4. Shift in Our Relationship with Time

It is a defining characteristic of rationalist, Enlightenment thinking to make time a measureable and therefore a scarce resource. Other cultures see time as infinite rather than scarce and cyclical rather than linear. We tend to regard natural resources as infinite and time as limited when, if anything, it is the other way round.

This shift encourages us to change the way we pay attention to 'things' and to see and to manage flows rather than stocks, process rather than structure. As Heraclitus said: everything flows.

Time also has different qualities. We appreciate that sometimes it flies by; other times it drags. We can learn to appreciate the qualities of time, in particular the distinction between clock time (called *chronos*) and the notion of the right time, the fateful time, the time that feels right for an initiative or a significant move (called *kairos*). Practitioners of transformative innovation will also be familiar with the notion of 'now or never' time, the entrepreneurial moment, the 'moment of truth'.

Taking a cyclical view of time helps us to shift the way we think about endings, which are always an echo of our fear of death. We need to complete, to close well – understanding that this is what makes space for the next cycle. This shift in perspective pays attention to endings as much as beginnings ('start-ups'), hospice work for the dying culture as much as midwifery for the new.

5. *From Fragmentation to Wholeness*

The rationalist, Enlightenment perspective breaks complex systems down into discrete parts in order to understand them. This shift requires a perspective that equally favours holism, 'joining up', connection, seeing things in patterns rather than in isolation. These are not alternatives but complementary views. Like structure and process, we cannot appreciate the one without the other. The ideal is 'holism with focus'.

This is the thinking behind Tony Hodgson's world system model, a pattern of twelve interconnected nodes each of which needs to be viable in its own right for the system overall to be healthy. The model is the basis for the IFF World Game in which groups are invited to explore an issue (focus) in the context of this web of interconnected systems under stress (holism) in order to find a way through to wise systemic action. We cannot analyse our way through this level of complexity, but we can play with it.

Christopher Alexander, in his book *A Pattern Language*, talks of 'laws of wholeness' – which provide a very different approach to notions of 'scale' and 'growth'. Alexander writes from the perspective of architecture and urban design, but his insights into patterns of relationship between parts and wholes apply much more widely. Given that much of the activity of organisations, for example, consists of a series of separate initiatives or projects, it can be helpful to think of them as contributing to the wholeness of the organisation and the wider whole of its relationship with the surrounding community.

Ultimately the whole is contained in the part, and vice versa. We see the universe in a grain of sand. Arthur Koestler's idea of 'holarchy' set out in *The Ghost in the Machine* suggests that every part (a holon) of a larger whole looks Janus-like in two directions: it has both a tendency towards integration and towards autonomy.

Those characteristics will be evident at any level of the organisation. The nature of the struggle between integration and autonomy in the Boardroom will be mirrored all the way through the organisation.

Finally, the shift from fragmentation to wholeness is also about meaning. Without some conception of wholeness, fragmentation leads to a loss of meaning, a world that no longer makes sense. Story is a powerful way of making wholes from disparate parts, weaving elements together to provide an instinctively satisfying sense of coherence. That is why the political battle today is less about ideas and more about shaping the narrative: it is the overarching stories we tell that influence how we see the world and the actions we regard as appropriate within it.

Together these five principles offer generous prompting to expand our rationalist, Enlightenment consciousness to embrace other ways of knowing, thinking and making sense of the world and our place in it. In truth these perspectives were equally present in the 18th century – they were simply drowned out by more powerful voices. To restore our effectiveness in action we need to reclaim them.

Two Loops

The 'Love and Fear Loops' emerged out of a conversation at Schumacher College on the day after the 9/11 attacks in the US when the entire student and faculty body gathered to try to make sense of what had happened. They were introduced into IFF by Brian Goodwin, who was there that day.

They usefully evoke the first two principles above: the distinction between a subject-object and a subject-subject reading of the world and the expansion of knowledge this enables. They help us to embrace complexity by revealing that love and fear are not simply ways of *being* in the world but also ways of *knowing* it.

The control loop: one way of being in the world is based on knowing by gaining control. In this mode we seek to understand the world by regarding everything as an object, standardised and categorised so that we can treat similar phenomena as being essentially the same. That makes all sorts of things possible, including 'objective' measurement. The problem is that human beings do not take kindly to being treated this way. So this approach often leads to alienation, which in turn demands even more control. Driving this self-reinforcing cycle are anxiety, insecurity and fear.

The participation loop: an alternative way of being in the world is based on knowing through participation, experiential knowledge. We can simply accept and acknowledge complexity and the unknown as an inevitable fact of modern life and instead of trying to avoid or control it, participate in it. Relish diversity, welcome surprises, look for the ineffable and appreciate the richness and the unique quality of all things. Such an embrace engenders a sense of belonging and reinforces the motivation to participate. Driving this reinforcing cycle are love, empathy, compassion and relationship.

On one level the loops simply remind us always to be alert to both the categorical and 'objective' knowledge obtained by gaining control and the experiential and 'subjective' knowledge gained through participation. But the use of the more emotive terms 'love' and 'fear' points to the deeper insights of enactive cognition developed by Francisco Varela, Evan Thompson and Eleanor Rosch in *The Embodied Mind*. This view suggests that who we are in the world conditions how the world occurs to us, how it rises up to meet us. Time and again the truth of this perspective is confirmed in our daily lives and conversation where we are far more likely to see what we believe than to believe what we see.

Both the 'love and participation' and the 'fear and control' responses are always available to us. The challenge for those of us raised to control what we don't understand is to get them in the right balance. In confused and novel situations we need to ensure that the culture of control finds its place within a culture of participation, rather than vice versa. For it is in the participation cycle that we find our creativity, energy and the hidden human resources we need to cope with the unprecedented. Disappointment and withdrawal can draw us into the fear loop, hope and play can lead us out of it.

Some readers will recognise in the two loops echoes of Adam Kahane's exploration of *Power and Love: a theory and practice of social change*. This is a book inspired by Martin Luther King's observation in a speech in 1967 that "Power without love is reckless and abusive and love without power is sentimental and anaemic… This collision of immoral power with powerless morality constitutes the major crisis of our time."

King's mentor, Paul Tillich, defines power as "the drive of everything living to realise itself, with increasing intensity and extensity", while love is "the drive towards the unity of the separated". Adam suggests that, just as we need to pay attention to the two ways of knowing inherent in the love and fear loops, so we must likewise be aware of these fundamental drives. He likens this to walking on two legs – first one, then the other, never veering too far from the path we must all tread between reckless and abusive power and sentimental and anaemic love.

A Variety of Prompts

We have found it helpful to encapsulate some of the significant shifts in perspective discussed in this chapter in a series of prompts that can help nudge us out of familiar patterns and invite us to 'try other worldviews on for size'. These prompts suggest what we might look for, appreciate, value, pay attention to, how we might behave, show up, take action – beyond our stock responses and repertoire.

Some speak to how we conduct ourselves – 'Be fun to be around', for example. Others offer insight on how to operate in a complex human system, engaging the other – 'Tolerate differences in order to discover richer wholeness' or 'Do not let our values limit our circle of empathy'.

Some suggest a reverse of the usual priorities – 'Privilege the science of qualities over the science of quantities', for example, or 'Don't look for the edge, find the centre'. There are managerial prompts for dealing with complex systems – 'Disperse responsibility', or 'Facilitate self-organisation'. Liberating prompts: 'Dance, space, movement, do something risky', or 'Seek playful forms that generate serious results'. And then there are the downright enigmatic, such as my personal favourite – 'Climb the mountain that isn't there'.

All of these prompts are derived from IFF's early experience in seeking to take on complex, messy problems in the real world. Each was originally written as a way of encapsulating what we had learned from research and discussion in a form that might guide and develop our own practice.

It turned out that these prompts were equally valued by the people we were working with. So we have since made them up into a pack of 52 cards (there are also two blank jokers that are intended to evoke the energy of the trickster or the wise fool). People naturally invent games to play with them. Strategy poker, for example, or the prompt card Tarot reading. Many people keep a set on their desk for inspiration in difficult moments or to suggest new angles on challenges they are working on during the day.

Some of those we have worked with have devised their own prompts, derived from their own transformative projects, as reminders of what they have learned, orientations for newcomers to the organisation and wisdom to return to when times get hard.

Further Reading – details at www.iffpraxis.com/ti

Ten Things to do in a Conceptual Emergency

Imagining Social Change

Chapter 2 was about how to make sense of the modern world. This one suggests how we might imagine and design effective action to address the challenges and sense of unease we experience when we do so.

It starts from the recognition that we are social creatures, living in a pattern of relationships with others. So it is important that we get a collective sense of the landscape we inhabit and the breadth and depth of different perspectives that exist, even in one small organisation, about how the world is going, what needs to change, what needs to stay the same.

Equally, we need to recognise that this diversity of views does not go away simply because the group has agreed on a 'vision statement': we will in practice have to continue to take these multiple perspectives into account – to say nothing of the wider world of events and other actors – as we steer our own course into the future.

We have found Three Horizons to be a powerful and intuitive framework for convening an open conversation about the past, the present and the future; a conversation that sets the ground for effective action – transformative innovation. Further, treating tensions and arguments along the way as dilemmas (see page 52) rather than as simple choices provides useful beacons to help pilot an innovative project into the future.

Three Horizons and Social Change

Three Horizons is a framework for understanding the process of social change. At its simplest we can see it as describing three patterns of activity and how their interactions play out over time. The framework maps a shift from the established patterns of the first horizon to the emergence of new patterns in the third, via the transition activity of the second.

The **first horizon** – H1 – describes the dominant systems in place now. It represents 'business as usual'. We rely on these systems being stable and reliable: the trains running on time, the lights coming on when we flick the switch and so on. But as the world changes, so aspects of 'business as usual' begin to feel out of place, unsustainable or no longer fit for purpose. Eventually 'business as usual' will always be superseded by new ways of doing things.

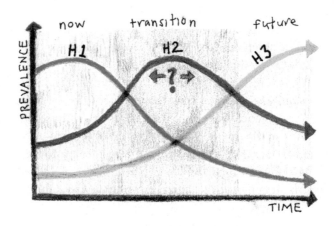

The **third horizon** – H3 – emerges as the long-term successor to 'business as usual'. It grows from fringe activity in the present that introduces completely new ways of doing things which turn out to be much better fitted to the world that is emerging than the dominant H1 systems.

The **second horizon** – H2 – is a pattern of transition activities and innovations, people trying things out in response to the ways in which the landscape is changing. Some of these innovations will be absorbed into the H1 systems to prolong their life (we call them H2 minus: H2-) while some will pave the way for the subsequent emergence of the radically different H3 systems (these are called H2 plus: H2+).

As the framework with its three lines suggests, all three horizons are always present. Aspects of H1 will persist in any new 'business as usual'. Aspects of H3 are always evident, if not obvious, in current discourse and argument and in all kinds of activity on the fringes of the dominant system. And H2, like a moving border between past and future, is all around us in examples of innovative alternative practice.

But the first horizon's commitment is to survival. The dominant system can maintain its dominance even in a changing world either by crushing second and third horizon innovation, or by co-opting it to support the old system.

These behaviours lead to variants on the smooth transition depicted on the previous page (these variants are illustrated overleaf). One is the 'collapse and recovery' scenario in which more and more resource is invested in a first horizon system that eventually fails, starving the second and third horizons in the process and delaying the transition.

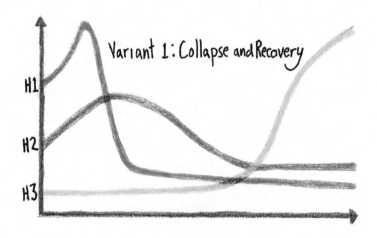

More common in the public and social sectors is the 'capture and extension' scenario in which innovations in H2 are 'mainstreamed' in order to prolong the life of the existing system against the grain of a changing world.

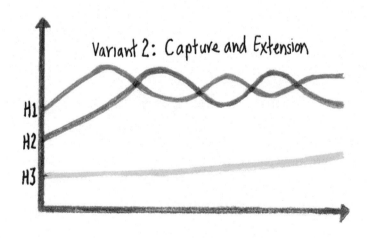

The Three Horizons framework offers a simple way into a conversation about:

- the dominant system (horizon 1) and the challenges to its sustainability into the future, i.e. the case for change.

- the aspirational future state, the ideal system we desire and of which we can identify elements in the present that give us encouragement and inspiration (horizon 3).

- the nature of the tensions and dilemmas between H3 vision and H1 reality, and the subtle processes of change, new ways of working, new capacities, new structures even, required to navigate the transition between them.

- developing a mature perspective that accepts the need *both* to address the challenges to the first horizon *and* nurture the seeds of the third. This is not an either/or, good/bad discussion. We need to keep the plane in the air whilst redesigning it so that it is fit for the different circumstances of the emerging future.

Convening the Future

Bill Sharpe's book *Three Horizons: the patterning of hope* expands in detail on how working with this framework encourages a number of central practices. The first is to *see things as patterns*, to think systemically. The framework draws our attention towards systemic patterns rather than individual events or global trends. These patterns result from the activity and behaviour of those who are maintaining or creating them in the present.

That includes ourselves: we need to *put ourselves in the picture*. We are also actors and can choose which patterns we want to maintain and which we want to shift. Because you are reading this book you likely have some aspiration to transform the dominant H1 system in some way. That will be a specific desire, not a comprehensive one: you might be happy to maintain a functioning transport system, for example, or the pattern of relationships that enables you to hold this book in your hand or to read it on your device, even while working to transform other aspects of society like healthcare or the prison system.

We all embrace all three perspectives in our lives – conventional in some areas, entrepreneurial in others, and visionary usually in those areas we care about the most. The third horizon in the present is a pattern of activity pursued by people driven by their values, doing something they believe in, making a stand in one area of their lives.

It is possible to *convene the future* by listening out for and becoming adept at managing a conversation between the 'voices' of all three horizons. The three horizons are not simply expressions of time – short, medium and long term. Each horizon in effect is developing a different quality already existing in the present, and which might become more prominent depending on how people choose to act – to maintain the familiar or pioneer the new. It is these three different qualities, three appreciations of 'the future potential of the present moment' that can be heard in a Three Horizons conversation.

The H1 voice is the voice of the *manager*. It talks about maintaining the current system and usually expresses concern. The H2 voice is the voice of the *entrepreneur*. It talks about trying something different and often expresses a combination of urgency and frustration. The H3 voice is the voice of the *visionary*. It talks about dreams and deep aspirations and is usually both humble and inspiring.

A Three Horizons conversation brings all of these voices into play – as they are expressed by different people and by ourselves. On the next page, Jennifer Williams's table of typical exchanges between the three 'mindsets' (fixed and usually negative) and 'perspectives' (open and usually positive) provides a helpful guide to what to expect in this conversation in practice. 'Convening the future' means becoming aware of all of these perspectives and working with them to shift the conversation in a generative direction.

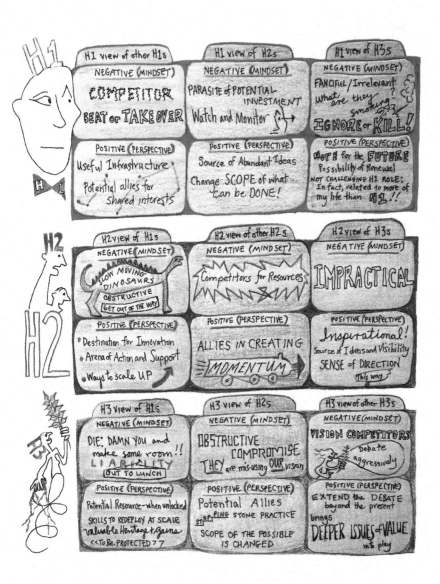

Convening this conversation in practice can take many different forms. A simple questionnaire asking people to identify causes for concern (H1), aspirations for the future (H3), hope, encouragement and inspiration in the present (H3 in the present) and promising innovations in play (H2) can be useful, particularly as a way of getting a rough view of a new group's Three Horizons landscape around a subject area. The results can be mapped on a Three Horizons chart and then fed back to the group when it meets in person – as a basis for expanding the conversation from there.

Another approach is simply to facilitate the conversation and record it on a Three Horizons chart. The important rule here is to guide people through the conversation in the order H1, H3, H2. Moving from H1 to H3 is what opens the space for imaginative thinking in H2.

We have found that it is helpful to prompt this conversation by introducing the three domains of the changing world, changing people (staff, clients, families, demographics, etc.) and changing policy and practice in the area in question. A series of statements to prompt the conversation to cover these domains can help to keep things focused. Feeding in content in this way can also make sure the conversation does not ignore the difficult issues that are typically not talked about (elephants in the room), or the wider global context that might otherwise appear irrelevant.

Following an initial open conversation, the next step is to process the results to identify an action plan appropriate for the twin tasks of 'redesigning the plane whilst flying it'.

This is different from simply brainstorming good ideas for innovation. The Three Horizons conversation will have given people a sense of the distinction between H2- and H2+ innovation and the task is to design a portfolio that covers both. The H1 manager is likely to be looking for 'sustaining innovation' – to improve the existing system, make it more efficient, smarter, faster, cheaper, safer and so on. The H2 entrepreneur will be more opportunistic, up for trying new things just to see what effect they might have on the system – 'disruptive innovation'. The H3 visionary is looking for 'transformative innovation' – seeking to shift the system intentionally in the direction of his or her aspirations.

With regard to the last, the initial Three Horizons conversation will have started to reveal not only an aspirational vision of a third horizon pattern very different from the first, but also examples of aspects of this new culture already present at some scale. These examples give hope and encouragement that the third horizon can be realised. Transformative innovation seeks to build on such examples: to embody a new pattern in the present around which other resources can assemble, growing over time a new pattern of viability for the system as a whole.

This is a point where IFF prompts (see page 41) can be used to evoke the H3 imagination. They help us to imagine the qualities of visionary, H2+ initiatives that can effectively challenge and establish themselves in dominant H1 cultures of thinking and acting.

One common feature is to start on a small scale, but with something that is authentically representative of the H3 culture imagined and that ideally might have a systemic effect. The metaphor of 'social acupuncture' suggests a small action that is delivered in just the right place at the right time to have positive impacts ripple through the system. Others talk of 'picking the lock' that opens up the system and releases H1 resources to operate in new ways. Both metaphors conjure up images of delicate instruments, carefully applied.

IFF has developed a Kit to support both phases of the Three Horizons conversation. It contains domain-specific cards (changing world, changing people, changing policy and practice) and a simple set of instructions – which can be downloaded as a separate resource. It is designed to help any group facilitate its own Three Horizons conversation in order to get a sense of the emerging landscape of present concerns, future aspirations and ambiguous innovation as it occurs to the people concerned and subsequently to make sense of that conversation as the basis for a comprehensive innovation plan.

Dilemmas

Thinking in terms of dilemmas (where we need to think both/and rather than make a simple either/or choice) can be helpful in designing a transformative innovation initiative and for piloting it through the turbulent transition towards the future.

Dilemma thinking was pioneered by the management theorist Charles Hampden-Turner and has been substantially developed in practice by Tony Hodgson. The characteristic of a dilemma is that it tugs us between two positive values where a simple choice is inadequate. We want *both* structure *and* freedom, for example, or a job that gives us *both* money *and* meaning. If we place these values not at different ends of a spectrum but at right angles, we create a 'dilemma space' with a sweet spot (top right corner) in which we can combine the best of *both* values – where we can have our cake and eat it.

We are likely to find the Three Horizons conversation populated by many such dilemmas. There will be tensions between the H1 business-as-usual system and the aspirational third horizon. The first horizon works, the third horizon liberates – both good things. There will almost certainly be value tensions in the wider world, even if they have not shown up in the initial conversation. A group seeking to shift global capitalism to a new pattern of compassion and inclusion, for example, will sooner or later have to reckon with others in the world applying their resources and energy to competing H3 visions. We cannot ignore other voices and other perspectives.

Even if we are aligned around an aspirational vision of the third horizon, tensions are likely to arise about the best means to gain that end. Should we rely on the market or on state regulation to solve obesity, for example, and should our actions privilege local choice or global efficacy? Dilemmas abound, even when we are aligned on purpose.

Effective strategy, policy and action needs to confront these dilemmas in the transition zone rather than evade or succumb to them.

Most dilemmas take a similar form. There is generally a 'rock value' with the quality of the immovable object on one horn, and a 'whirlpool value' with the quality of an irresistible force on the other. If we cling exclusively to either, then the other will find us out eventually. Thus a business might fail as easily by sticking rigidly to its core product as it might by putting all of its resources into speculative innovation: this is a dilemma, not a choice, and needs to be managed as such.

One core dilemma that is ever present is between focus and holism, between being for oneself and being for the whole. As John Cage expressed it in his *Lecture on Nothing*: "Structure without life is dead; and life without structure is unseen." If you cannot find any other dilemmas in the landscape then look for that one: it will be there.

Moving towards the resolution space in the top right hand corner, where 1 + 1 = 3, is not a simple linear process. It is like tacking a sailing boat against the wind. We may need to move towards the rock value for a while, before turning to introduce more of the whirlpool value.

This is the smart H2+ policy course, consciously steering a path between two poles and using the tension between them as a source of propulsion, a motive force to determine the direction of travel towards the creative resolution of the third horizon.

There are five possible outcomes in managing a dilemma. If we stick to the rock value we will become a dinosaur and die out. If we stick to the whirlpool value we become a unicorn – a mythical beast. If we compromise we end up as an ostrich, head in the sand. If we get stuck in the zone of conflict we will be like Dr Doolittle's push-me-pull-you. But if we get to the resolution space we will soar like an eagle.

To work through the critical dilemmas identified in the Three Horizons conversation it is helpful to divide the dilemma space into five zones, corresponding to the zones shown in the graphic on the next page. Then for the tension in question we can perform the following step-by-step analysis, working through the zones in order:

- Zone 1: State what is essential from this perspective. What would we do if we privileged this perspective?

- Zone 2: State what is essential from this perspective. What would we do if we privileged this perspective?

- Zone 3: What are the typical activities that arise from a compromise between the two values? How is the tension between them typically managed in practice?

- Zone 4: Where are the values in conflict? What are the (unresolved) arguments that currently take place between them?

- Zone 5: Seek creative resolution: what can the Zone 1 value offer the Zone 2 value without loss of integrity, and vice versa?

What this exercise quickly brings out is the following:

- It is very easy to identify compromise solutions that suppress the tension without addressing it (zone 3). It is much more difficult to get to the resolution space (zone 5).

- A willingness to wrestle with and 'ride the horns' of the dilemma in zone 4 prevents the slip into easy compromise, or the tendency to migrate to either pole of the discussion.

- It is interesting to find that wrestling with the dilemma and seeking creative ways to get the best of both worlds often reveals existing practice that can now be seen in a new light – exemplifying the third horizon in the present. "The future is already here, just unevenly distributed" – but we first have to know what we are looking for.

Imaginary Islands

One of the IFF Prompt Cards (see page 41) tells us to 'develop a future consciousness to inform the present'. The Three Horizons framework helps us to do just that: in fact, to recognise our future consciousness as being integral to our appreciation of the present moment. We can see in our circumstances today the potential for crisis and decline, for opportunity and innovation, and for the visionary realisation of our highest aspirations.

We have a choice about which we choose to privilege in any moment, in any situation, which we choose to embody in our lives and thus contribute to the pattern of other lives. Bill Sharpe's book argues for the intentional development of this capacity for 'future consciousness' as a *societal* capacity, like language. In a visionary final chapter he offers four 'imaginary islands' that we as a society might use as shared beacons to guide us into the future.

The image comes from the story of Polynesian sailors who can navigate great distances without recourse to instruments. They are adept at reading the wind, tides, the sun and the stars. They also take bearings on visible landmasses, using one island then another as beacons and waymarks.

But most remarkable is their practice when there are no islands. In that case they just imagine them, and take a bearing accordingly. As Bill puts it: "These are not visions of the destination, nor are they pathways, but they help hold all of the subtle indicators together in the minds of the sailors such that a true way may be found. The placing and pattern of these islands and their relationship to observable phenomena is a shared cultural form passed across the generations."

What imaginary islands might help us keep our bearings in the course of both designing and implementing transformative innovation? Bill has four suggestions:

The first is *abundance*. Life is always a configuration of abundance, even as individual lives might experience scarcity. The first horizon has become dominant because it has learned to configure a source of abundance, and begins to fail when that resource starts to deplete. The third horizon will configure a new source of abundance.

The second is *infinite diversity*. This flows from the first – life configures abundance in endlessly evolving patterns of change, variation and diversity. All evolution is co-evolution: each change in one pattern, in one organism, opens up possibility for change in other parts of the ecosystem. The depth of interaction drives more growth, more diversity, ever more complex patterns. The third horizon will emerge from creative engagement with this complexity rather than its denial.

The third is *mutuality*. As noted earlier, there are qualities of life that can only be held in common. They are neither qualities in the individual nor in the whole, but in the combination of both. We are navigating towards a third horizon in which we recognise that our aspirations will be realised not in ourselves alone but in a social pattern, a society, that sustains the mutual qualities of life we desire.

The fourth island is the most dimly discerned of all: *the patterning of hope*.

Further Reading – details at www.iffpraxis.com/ti

Three Horizons: the patterning of hope

Transformative Innovation in Education: a playbook for pragmatic visionaries (includes a chapter on dilemmas)

Three Horizons Kit for Transformative Innovation: a guide for users

The Human System

One of the lessons from previous chapters is that in order to act effectively in a complex world we need to put ourselves, our humanity, in the picture. We are agents in the world: active, embodied sense-makers with heads, hearts, hands, souls and psyches, living our lives in a pattern of other lives.

However sophisticated our analysis of complex systems we must remember that, ultimately, when we seek to act on them we will be doing so with a group of people. However compelling an idea, likewise it will tend to show up in practice embodied in a more or less attractive or persuasive advocate.

We are always and inevitably dealing with human systems and, as Geoffrey Vickers told us earlier, "human systems are different". One way in which they are different is that symptoms of overload and confusion are going to manifest in significant – and largely unconscious - psychological responses.

Maureen O'Hara, who worked alongside Carl Rogers for three decades and has been an invaluable guide for IFF in the ways of the human system, identifies three typical patterns of response. One is a *neurotic* response: an obsession with control and predictability, denial of the confusion by looking for simple answers, retreat to various forms of fundamentalism and the powerful reassertion of old beliefs. This is a reactionary response, seeking comfort in past certainties.

There is also a more disintegrative response. This might be described as *psychotic*: giving up on making effective sense of the world, nihilism, dissociation, dropping out, seeking release in alcohol or drugs, 'eat, drink and be merry', tuning out.

There is ample evidence for both responses in today's world. They are both coping strategies. They can help for a while, but they can equally be destructive and dysfunctional – for the individual, for organisations and for society. Neither is capable of rising to the demands the world now makes on us or of grasping the abundant opportunities it offers.

To realise the full benefits, opportunities and potential of living in the modern world we need to explore a third response. This is the *transformative* response, based on learning, adaptation and growth: taking ownership of our internal world, making new meaning within changing realities, understanding people and cultures at a human level, and encouraging others to do likewise. As Carl Jung said, "we don't solve our problems, we outgrow them".

It is instructive to overlay these patterns of neurotic denial, psychotic collapse and generative growth on the Three Horizons framework discussed in the previous chapter. The patterns described there also live in human systems – and the waning of first horizon certainties in particular will raise psychological as well as rational defences, many of them wholly unconscious. There is no easy answer to these challenges: simply to remember that, whatever else is going on, there is a human system at its heart – whole persons living in a pattern of relationship with others.

This chapter offers three essential orientations towards working with the human system in the pursuit of transformative innovation: organising for action, managing the process, and sustaining the people involved.

Organising for Action

Deciding to initiate transformative innovation is not a simple, mechanical process. It is likely to spring first from a general sense of uneasiness with existing patterns of activity and a growing feeling that, even with improvement, they are becoming unsustainable and fundamentally unable to provide for much longer the life-enhancing qualities we value.

That concern inevitably also triggers an aspiration, whether or not it can be articulated at this stage: the imagining of a new pattern that would realise these cherished qualities of life again in the circumstances of a changing world.

What to do with this feeling? It may be that you decide to 'convene the future' in a Three Horizons conversation (see page 47) to explore whether or not you are alone in your concerns about the unsustainability of the first horizon and to see how widely your aspirations for transition to a different future are shared.

Through the process (whether it be in a Three Horizons conversation or simply in other informal contacts with colleagues and peers) your aspiration will start to be shared, shaped and nurtured by a small number of other individuals who find it inspiring.

It is this energy that will initiate action. This small group, with the strength of their shared commitment and belief, provides a new point of stability in the system, around which a different pattern of activity can emerge and develop.

We call this group a 'creative integrity'. It is a distinctive organisational form. The people involved are not configured around a project plan, or a budget, or their formal roles, or the direction of the senior manager or 'leader'. They are configured around commitment – the commitment of a small group (it may start with just two people, so long as there is more than one) who are ready to take a stand for a new way of working, to demonstrate through their actions that another way is possible, to express a part of their third horizon aspirational selves.

This is an integrity because it is an expression of wholeness and relationship. It is like a seed: it contains within it all that it will become. It is a living structure that like other living structures can only remain alive by sustaining its wholeness – its integrity. It is a manifestation in the present, an embodiment, of the third horizon potential of the present moment. That is why it is also 'creative': it distinguishes itself from the dominant culture, steps outside the existing patterns to stand for something different.

Margaret Mead famously told us not to doubt "that a small group of thoughtful, committed citizens can change the world; indeed, it's the only thing that ever has". But in order to do so they need to operate as a creative integrity. This is an insight inspired by Martin Albrow's work, alluded to in Chapter 2, on integrity as a distinct organisational form.

He suggests that an integrity can be formed by any group of people come together to maintain a sense of values-based purpose over time. It is this sense of purpose and values that holds the entity together rather than any formal constitution, hierarchical organisation chart or set of black letter rules. It is more like a family, a social movement or a group of friends than a corporation or even a members' club.

Individual participants each make their own contribution and are sustained in ways that they need through the integrity. The emerging results of their collective endeavours ripple through ever wider cycles of involvement. The entity self-organises, coordinated by the shared sense of purpose individually interpreted. And the entity in turn is constantly negotiating its relationship with other entities and with a changing external world.

In effect the integrity is navigating the fundamental dilemma identified in the previous chapter – between autonomy and integration, being for itself and being for the whole, between focus and holism.

The creative integrity manages this tension between concern for itself and concern for the whole along two dimensions of being and doing.

The 'being' axis can be seen as having *sovereignty* at one end – the ownership and control of resources of all kinds – and *recognition* at the other – how the entity is regarded, its reputation, the identity it has in the eyes of others.

The 'doing' axis has *agency* at one end – the capacity to get things done, to realise something in the world – and *reciprocity* at the other – a web of relationships and mutual obligations.

As a template for organising (rather than a static 'organisation') this framework allows any group, at any scale, effectively to create in the relationships between them the pattern (the integrity) to stick together and to get things done – without relying on formal organisational structures or a traditional 'leader'.

By periodically checking in on the four dimensions of sovereignty, recognition, reciprocity and agency it is possible to maintain a sense of the health of the integrity and to identify and address any imbalances or disturbances that occur, any feeling of being 'out of integrity'. This is especially important as the integrity, the initial small group, starts to grow.

If it is successful, this creative integrity will begin to attract other people to it. If it can be maintained, then (in tune with the notion of 'co-evolution' expressed earlier) other resources will begin to be drawn into the new patterning that it enables. Its actions will start to be recognised in the wider world. Its distinctive way of being, the new culture that it represents, will start to become visible to others and will form relationships with other parts of the system. At all stages it will need to remain aware of its own integrity, in order to ensure that its true potential is not lost or distorted in these new interactions.

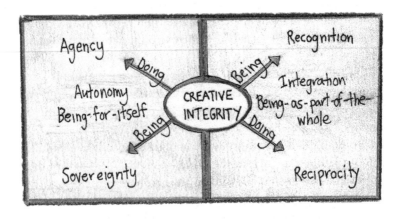

The Creative Integrity (Bill Sharpe after Martin Albrow)

This is the process of transformation – creating a new pattern to replace the old. We can see the first horizon as a **'patterned integrity'** – a set of mutually reinforcing activities that maintain a stable system, something that we can rely on. But there comes a time when people can no longer fully express themselves within this patterned integrity and we must then exercise our **'creative integrity'** to bring new patterns of life into existence.

BEING

As Bill Sharpe puts it: "Exercising creative integrity is the only way to bring the second and third horizons into existence, because it is the way we realise the possibilities in the unknown future". The goal of our transformative innovation is to establish a new, stable, 'patterned integrity' – a third horizon as reliable as the first.

Managing the Process

Managing a creative integrity, holding a culture and growing a practice into a space provided by new conceptual thinking, needs an approach more subtle and sophisticated than simple project management. The task requires the varied skills and competencies – in knowing, doing, being – of the producer.

This is a role most evident in the arts where it has been examined and championed in ground-breaking work from the Jerwood Charitable Foundation conducted by Kate Tyndall. Her book *The Producers: Alchemists of the Impossible* provides a series of rich interviews with arts producers in many disciplines and gives a flavour of the range of skills and attributes involved. The producer's role is essentially to mediate between the creative artists on the one hand and the structures of funding and accountability on the other in order to deliver an act of the imagination that is (by definition) unique and original.

This same underlying challenge also perfectly describes the practice of transformative innovation. For that reason IFF has engaged with Kate Tyndall and others to understand better how the producer competencies express themselves in the public, voluntary and social sectors, the domains of social innovation.

The fullest exploration can be found in the pamphlet *The Producer Role and the Art of the Impossible* drawing on the practice of Helen Marriage, Director of Artichoke. This describes seven lessons on how to act like a producer:

1. Don't start from 'this is impossible'
2. There are no rules (even where there are rules)
3. Get the fears articulated
4. Make friends
5. Take responsibility and seek contribution
6. Don't ask for permission – it cannot be given
7. Push the ambition.

Alongside these sit eight characteristics of the culture she inspires and embodies:

1. The culture is respectful
2. The culture is trusting
3. The culture is responsible
4. The culture is meticulous
5. The culture expects surprises
6. The culture demands quality
7. The culture promotes freedom
8. The culture feeds hope.

These brief headlines are included here simply as a taster for the full pamphlet. But even from these short notes it should be possible to get a feeling for the way the producer needs to operate to maintain a creative integrity, to nurture its own culture and to help it negotiate and form productive relationships with other actors. Certainly we have much to learn from the world of the arts. But equally the most successful transformative innovators we come across in the public and social sectors embody and enact many of these same characteristics.

IFF has also had the privilege over the years of working closely with Watershed, the cultural cinema and digital creativity hub in Bristol; in particular with Creative Director Clare Reddington and Managing Director Dick Penny, both exceptional producers.

Watershed has taken the producer skills to heart and has effectively become producer for the city, or certainly for its most creative and ground-breaking projects. It consciously sits in the second horizon space configuring people and resources in disciplined processes to bring third horizon imaginings into being. Unsurprisingly its skills and approach are now in demand around the world – and IFF has learned a lot from its practice. The pamphlet *Producing the Future: Watershed's role in ecosystems of cultural innovation* is a good introduction to the theory and practice of how an organisation itself can take on the producer role – and is discussed in more detail in Chapter 7.

Sustaining the People

We are all exercising our creative choices at an individual level all the time. But few of us are willing to take the existential risk of taking a stand on behalf of society. That is what forming a creative integrity implies.

The iconic picture is of the lone student with his shopping bag standing in front of a line of tanks descending on Tiananmen Square in 1989. Or Václav Havel's extraordinary essay, *The Power of the Powerless*, in which he invites fellow citizens suffering under a totalitarian regime not to protest or to dissent but simply to straighten their backbone, assert their human dignity and to 'live in truth'. These are examples of the assertion of new patterns of human potential and possibility inside systems that are closing down the space for them.

Whilst in the field of transformative innovation we are not usually talking about toppling a dictatorial regime, nevertheless there is always a sense of existential danger involved. The unavoidable fact is that if we wish to change a culture we are going to have to do something counter-cultural. Aftab Omer talks of cultural leadership arising from small acts of 'creative transgression'. There is always a risk that the dominant system will react aggressively to suppress such acts. Which is why it is prudent always to follow Neville Singh's guidance: to act with tact (don't make the dominant system wrong), timing (wait for an opening before making any move) and titration (pay attention to dosage, don't push your luck).

Even with these precautions transformative innovation can be a stressful affair. It always reminds me of the story of the advertisement Ernest Shackleton put in *The Times* to recruit men for one of his Antarctic expeditions: "Men wanted for hazardous journey. Low wages, bitter cold, long hours of complete darkness. Safe return doubtful. Honour and recognition in event of success".

It turns out that the advert is likely apocryphal, yet still regularly appears in anthologies of the best advertising copy ever written. There is something refreshingly honest yet inspiring in its tone: it is a call to express our selves, our creative integrity.

But equally it points to the risks we are taking. It is human systems that transform, but only if there is dedicated support for them to do so. Everyone involved in the growing integrity around a transformative innovation will experience their own 'a-ha' moments when the shift in practice finally makes sense to them. People will have this experience at different times and in different ways but, for the culture to shift, everyone must have such a moment.

It is also clear that this moment can be accompanied by feelings of loss or regret. Change happens at a personal level and involves shedding one pattern of activity in order to discover another. This is when the tears can come. Individuals need to be held through the transition and a culture of peer support can help.

Ideally this should be a routine component. It is implicit in the role of the producer. But it can also be made explicit in a number of ways. Meetings should be conducted in a way that encourages reflection, honesty, listening and acknowledgement that each of the people involved has a life, hopes, fears and concerns that go way beyond the project, way beyond work.

The IFF Kitbag has proved to be useful for this purpose. It contains a number of resources to help create and maintain such a space – from simple breathing and mindfulness exercises, to a 'feelings' check-in using a colour card, to a talking stick to slow things down and ensure that everyone is truly heard.

John Ballatt and Penny Campling's wonderful book describes a culture of *Intelligent Kindness* in which people exhibit warmth, generosity, empathy and compassion whilst maintaining appropriate boundaries and safeguards to ensure reckless and inappropriate behaviours are proscribed. This is what we should be aiming for.

This personal aspect of transformative innovation is often overlooked, but it is critical. It is not a culture that just happens – it has to be intentionally designed in from the start. IFF has recently published a short guide on how to incorporate simple peer support processes and practices into day to day working: *Cultivating a Culture of Kindness.* It is essential reading for any group embarking on the hazardous journey of transformative innovation.

Further Reading – details at www.iffpraxis.com/ti

Dancing at the Edge: competence, culture and organisation in the 21st century

The Producer Role and the Art of the Impossible

Producing the Future: Watershed's role in ecosystems of cultural innovation

Cultivating a Culture of Kindness: a brief guide to peer support in the workplace

Beyond Survival: a short guide to pioneering in response to the present crisis

IFF Kitbag

Frameworks for Action

Initiating and growing transformative innovation is fundamentally a process of social learning. It is about a group of people forming a creative integrity and learning how to thrive in an operating environment that is not necessarily set up to support the new pattern of activity they are bringing into being.

It is helpful to conceive of the transformative initiative from the start as a learning process and to manage it accordingly. In IFF our principal guide has been Max Boisot. His insights on the political economy of knowledge and their expression in what he calls 'the information space' or i-space have been foundational and provide a secure framework for understanding effective transformative innovation as a learning process over time.

We have also drawn heavily on the work of Jim Ewing, a master guide, coach and artist who developed over many years an elegant set of interconnected maps, tools and processes for guiding people through change. They work by finding creative ways to tap into our sub-conscious – the hints, clues, guesses, slips of the tongue, unknowing and just making it up that emanate from some under-acknowledged part of ourselves. If you found yourself in a position where you did not know what to do, he might ask: 'So what would somebody do who knew what to do in these circumstances?', and you would be left wondering where you had found the answer. Because it turns out it is always in there somewhere.

Jim developed a set of conversational frameworks to handle the many contradictory emotions, anecdotes, facts, perspectives and behaviours that will arise both within ourselves and within a group when we embark on the process of change. Two of these frameworks have proven particularly relevant and effective in supporting the process of transformative innovation – Impacto (about enrolling others in your aspirations) and Implemento (about taking a step, making a move). Both are explored in more detail later in this chapter.

Social Learning

First, however, it is necessary to set the overall context as social learning. Max Boisot's information space (at least in its two-dimensional guise) is defined by two axes representing the codification of knowledge and its diffusion. It is based on the insight that the more a piece of knowledge is abstracted and codified the easier it is to share – like a chemical formula. But at the same time a lot of depth and context is lost in the codification process. Knowledge that sits low in the i-space tends to be personal, embodied, experienced. Higher in the i-space it is abstract and symbolic.

The social learning cycle based on these dimensions generates new ideas at bottom left (not well codified, not widely shared), sees them articulated and codified to some degree, is then able to broadcast and disseminate them to a wider audience, and then sees that knowledge absorbed into practice – and in the process become experienced again. Scanning this new practice, the new features in the landscape that have resulted from people acting on new ideas, can provoke further thoughts, generate more new ideas (bottom left) and so the cycle starts again.

This is a learning cycle. It most commonly breaks down with the difficulty of translating theory or policy or new ideas (codified and abstract knowledge) into practice. We call this process 'convergence' – abstract ideas will be more readily absorbed into practice when they resonate with what is already known at some level.

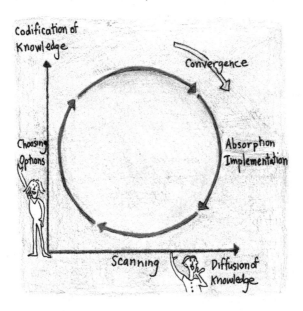

For effective absorption of new ideas into practice it is also helpful to keep the two contexts – where the ideas are generated and where they are eventually put into practice – as closely aligned as possible. Hence the virtue in starting small, applying a new idea with just a small group of people at first to see how it lands in practice before scanning the results, modifying the idea and then sharing it with a wider group.

Successive learning cycles will eventually lead to a workable form of the original idea being embedded in practice at a wide scale. This is the process described in the previous chapter – in which an initial creative integrity slowly expands by attracting new members, forming new relationships and eventually configuring enough of the system around it to create a new, stable pattern. The process is depicted below as three successive learning cycles – something Max calls 'the tricycle'.

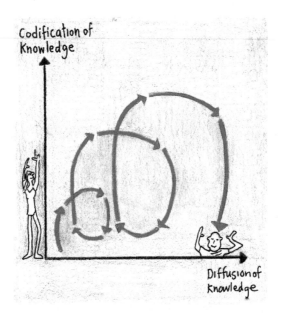

It is wise to make this explicitly a part of any strategy to put transformative innovation into practice, adopting an iterative process of journeys around the social learning cycle as the project progresses from year to year. Some projects – like the SHINE project (see page 21) – will set a day aside for learning and reflection at the end of each cycle.

That is also a good moment to check in on the Three Horizons conversation. How are the concerns in the first horizon developing, how are other second horizon innovations developing, how visible is your own transformative initiative becoming, how is the landscape changing? Incorporating this cycle of active reflection offers a learning-based approach to 'project management' and 'delivery'.

Learning can also be embedded in the initiative through regular action learning groups for those closely involved. These can incorporate peer support. There are many formats for such sessions. IFF favours a process that invites questions for insight rather than the giving and sharing of advice – evoking the capacities that lie at the edge of our competence and that a supportive environment might encourage us to explore.

Our personal learning through a transformative initiative will mirror the project learning: loosening old patterns, trying out new ones, establishing new competencies. Laying aside our power for a while in order to explore our edge.

The Buddhist and the Broker

The i-space also invites us to be more reflective about knowledge. Max was acutely aware of the richness that is lost in the process of codification just as much as the reach that is gained. One of his classic papers ('Organizational versus Market Knowledge: from concrete embodiment to abstract representation') contrasts the embodied knowledge possessed by a Zen master and the abstract, symbolic knowledge relied on by a bond analyst in the financial markets – 'the Buddhist and the broker'.

The broker operates entirely in the fast-paced world of abstraction and numbers in which the whole point of a market is that information is instantly and unambiguously available to all. The Buddhist by contrast shows a deep distrust of analytical reasoning as a way to gain valid knowledge of ultimate reality. His knowledge is embodied and can only be passed on slowly through face-to-face encounter. The Zen monk Dōgen said that he only really wanted one disciple, but he wanted him for a lifetime.

Personal commitment lies at the heart of creative integrity and imagined knowledge of the third horizon gives it its strength. So, transformative innovators should be aware that their journey around the social learning cycle is as likely to involve this process of personal resonance, apprenticeship and the sharing of experience low in the i-space as it is to involve the more conventional process of progressive codification and absorption.

Certainly there will be aspects that can be codified along the way – often into routines and practices that reinforce embodied experience. These moments of codification are more likely to emerge naturally as the integrity grows rather than formally at set points in the cycle.

Both readings of the learning cycle also point to the special significance of story or 'narrative knowledge' as an important half-way house between embodied, experiential knowledge and abstract, symbolic, codified data. Experiential knowledge of a situation is what you can see, hear, feel, smell, touch. Abstract symbolic knowledge is what you can extract from the situation that is stable or durable. Narrative knowledge is simply what you can say about it.

Max writes: "Narrative knowledge can be located somewhere in between fully embodied and fully abstract symbolic knowledge, to mediate the relationship between them. It partakes both of the expressiveness of the first and the symbolic reach of the second."

Transformative innovation will be working against the grain of a dominant culture and therefore probably against its traditional measures of 'success'. It also represents for the initial group involved a step into the unknown, a creative advance into novelty. Thus it is unlikely, especially in the early stages, that it will be able to generate codified, abstract data either to prove its effectiveness or to spread the practice. It is more likely that the practice will grow through observation and *resonance*, low in the i-space. And the most telling codification of impact or success will be the stories that can be told.

Taking Action

In 2010 IFF produced a Three Horizons Kit for Scottish schools to enable them to 'convene the future' (see page 47) amongst senior staff to discover the scope for transformative innovation afforded by the new policy of Curriculum for Excellence.

The Kit worked very effectively to elicit aspirations for the future, inspiration and encouragement in the present and diverse ideas for transformative innovation to bridge the gap between the two. The challenge was how to progress these new ideas in circumstances where there was little spare management capacity, no training budget, no time, no resources and certainly no consultants in support. We were asked whether we could develop another Kit to help get teachers into action and to guide them through the process of transformative change.

The request was tailor-made for Jim Ewing's suite of maps and tools. Of course there are countless other processes available for initiating and keeping things moving through change. But there is a simplicity, consistency and inter-relatedness in Jim's set of approaches that is attractive. Their underlying philosophy dovetails nicely with the Three Horizons framework and the five principles set out in Chapter 2. And as people who use them tell us over and over again: "this stuff really works".

The suite of tools derives from a fundamental insight that sets alongside the relationship between actions and results a broader reading of the landscape for change that embraces both the actions of others and other external forces and our own pattern of beliefs and assumptions about how the world works. That includes our beliefs and assumptions about change.

Accessing all of the tools and realising their full potential requires training from a licensed practitioner. But both Impacto and Implemento – which are described below – are largely intuitive and we found that they are very effective in the school setting, for example, with minimal coaching. Indeed, there is now a large body of teenagers in Scotland who are routinely applying these frameworks having experienced them at school. If they find themselves faced with a difficult decision their immediate thought is to 'implemento it'.

The notes below should provide enough information to allow you to develop at least a rudimentary practice with both of these tools, and perhaps encourage you to explore these and other tools in the set more deeply in the future.

Impacto

The Three Horizons conversation will provide the basis for a story of transformation, a journey from the safety of the first horizon towards the aspirations of the third. To move into action, it will help to be able to communicate this story convincingly for ourselves, and to enrol others whose support we might need.

Impacto provides a simple framework for drawing out that story. The framework has five elements. You can populate them in any order, depending on where your energy and inspiration lie, or what material you already have to hand. Don't worry about how the whole thing hangs together, just invent what seems right in each domain in response to the sample trigger questions listed below.

Purpose:
- *What are we up to? Why are we putting energy into this? How does it serve our aspirations? What values are we seeking to make more present in the world through this initiative?*

Urgency:
- *Why are we doing this now? What is the opportunity and how long will it last? What is the risk if we do nothing? What is wrong that needs changing?*

Destination:
- *What outcomes are we shooting for? What will our third horizon look and feel like? How will we be operating in the future as a result of this work? What changes in the world will we see? What will the good things already going on have evolved into?*

Success Path:
- *How will we get from our present state to the destination described? What are the stepping-stones to success? If we stand in the future with our vision achieved, how did we get from there to here?*

Commitment:
- *What are we willing to commit to this venture, as individuals and collectively? How important is it to us? How can others help and what do we need them to do?*

Jim learned that in telling the story it is important to do so in the order of the elements above – like climbing a staircase. If you start on one of the higher steps then you are likely to be drawn back down to the bottom by your audience in any event. It is common to start a pitch with the success path (I have a remarkable new gadget) and commitment (I need your investment). What the audience is likely to be thinking is more likely 'why is she telling me all this?' (purpose) or 'do we really have to talk about this now?' (urgency).

The story is structured like this so that there are opportunities to check for understanding and agreement at each stage. Don't move on to the next step until you have agreement, or feedback, on the present one. If there is no agreement on purpose it is best to talk about that, rather than gloss over it. If views about the success path differ then have that conversation – don't rush on to commitment, because it will not be forthcoming. Listen to people's reactions and input along the way in order to build agreement as you go.

The same will apply as the project progresses. The Impacto story provides a reference to revisit and rebuild as things go along, both for the group and the wider community.

It is worth saying a little more about the first and last elements. Jim says that "Purpose provides a foundation of meaning for the rest of the communication. If the purpose is unclear then the communication will be too. Purposes are the steadying forces on which the rest of the communication sits".

Commitment is equally fundamental: this part of the story is not just a request for resources but an expression of existing commitment in the team. As we have seen, in the case of transformative innovation the team's commitment may look slender in terms of time and money, but is in reality significant and unshakeable.

Implemento

Sooner or later, having enrolled others in your story, the time will come to make the first move, to get into action. But what kind of action? Certainly at the start of the process and likely at points along the way, there will be moments when there is a step to be taken, a move to be made, and you are not sure which way to go.

Implemento provides a framework for rehearsing potential moves ahead of time and redesigning them to maximise their chances of success and mitigate the risk of failure. The process starts from our best guess for an initiative we think might work. Since it is essentially a redesign conversation you can start with the vaguest idea of an initiative and the conversation will do the rest.

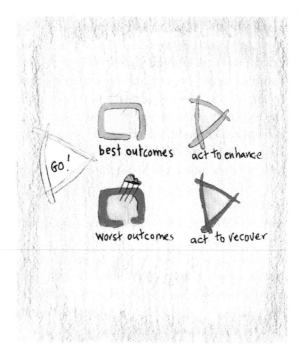

The first step is to imagine taking an initiative and then ask 'what is the worst that could happen?' That conversation draws out our unconscious, normally unstated, fears and brings the group to describe a place where the initiative has resulted in disastrous failure. Someone then feeds this story back as if it has actually happened. This moment can feel depressing. But it turns out we are much more creative problem solvers in adversity: we are better at addressing problems that have actually occurred than those that might lie in the future. The Implemento process allows us to draw on this natural capacity to be 'wise after the event'. It may take some time, but sooner or later the group will start to generate a serious programme of recovery steps – the things they would do to recover the situation if they really found themselves in this position.

Just as we can be tempted to keep our fears and concerns about failure to ourselves, so we are likely to self-censor our highest hopes for an initiative in order not to sound naïve and unrealistic. The Implemento framework mirrors the first part of the process by asking about highest hopes. That conversation brings the group to a place of best outcomes, international accolades and honours all round.

This is the moment again for someone to tell the story of this world as if it had happened – and to ask the group what they want to do next. What might they now do to build on this success? This is pushing into forbidden territory – beyond our highest hopes. But it turns out that every group has ideas about what to do once we get there.

The real skill lies in extracting the full value from this conversation. It will come as a surprise to the group to realise that their recovery steps have effectively re-designed the initiative. They may take a little tweaking, but if we want to avoid the worst outcomes then we should design in our recovery steps from the start. Typical steps may include rebuilding bridges with key stakeholder groups, for example – suggesting that it would be good to ensure those relationships are strong before you begin. Equally, the acts to enhance our best outcomes will also have provided clues about options to look out for so that we are not overwhelmed by runaway success. We will have contemplated how things might develop if they go really well and can now be ready for that.

Looking for emergent patterns across the best and worst outcomes will also reveal elements common to each. They can be used to generate a balanced scorecard of measures intrinsic to the initiative to keep track of our own aspirations and to reassure those in the first horizon. It is also possible to ask at this stage what an acceptable minimum outcome would be on each of these measures – effectively defining 'failure' in our own terms.

An Implemento conversation in one school was about trying out a new approach to parents' evenings. One worst fear was that nobody would come; the highest hope couldn't find a room big enough to hold the throng. Clearly attendance and engagement were measures of success for the initiative. Both extremes were unlikely. So what would be an acceptable minimum on a first outing for the new model? After some discussion it was agreed that if six people came that would at least be a start. Anything less would show that the idea was just not going to fly.

Without that conversation the teachers might have been thoroughly dispirited when only eight people came on the night. But this was above their threshold and so they chose to carry on. They had to think hard about how to improve things, for sure, but they were redesigning the initiative rather than abandoning it.

The great thing about Implemento is that it turns risk into 'managed risk' and encourages people to make a move that previously might have looked too scary: in other words, to be the adventurers they always wanted to be. It also works neatly with whatever energy is in the group, including the energy of opposition. When the first step in the conversation is to ask 'what is the worst that could happen?' and to treat the answers seriously, everyone becomes a participant.

We have found that Impacto and Implemento are simple and effective in nurturing transformative innovation as both practical hope and wise initiative. That was Jim's phrase and it has become the strapline for IFF.

The images of Impacto and Implemento in this chapter are copyright © 1989-2016 Executive Arts Limited www.executivearts.co.uk and redrawn with the copyright holder's permission.

Further Reading – details at www.iffpraxis.com/ti

IFF Practice Centre
Real World Change: Maps for the Journey

The previous chapters have provided guidance to practitioners of transformative innovation, those seeking to introduce and grow a new pattern of activity, a new culture, in the presence of the old. To the extent that the wider context has shown up in the story so far it is as a set of problems to be managed, dilemmas to be negotiated, circumstances to get unstuck.

Yet there are ways in which the wider context of policy, strategy and finance can actively contribute to a more fruitful landscape for transformative innovation. This is very much the ideal. First and third horizon energies can be harnessed in a mutual endeavour to transition mature systems over time to patterns that are likely to be more viable for the future.

But this is rare in practice, not least because a whole other set of public, political and social pressures apply at the level of policy and strategy – pressures that small-scale innovative initiatives can safely ignore. Whilst there is no shortage of literature on the practice of innovation, the interface between such innovation and existing infrastructural systems, and particularly the ways in which the two can support each other and develop in tandem, is less well researched. Which is why this chapter and the next may be the most important of all.

What is required is a policy framework for transition, something to enable a transition from one dominant mode of operation in a large, complex public system to another, over time, while ensuring that operations do not fail in the process. In other words, 'redesigning the plane whilst flying it', which appears today less like a party trick and more a core competence for the policymaker. There are five core components:

- A compelling vision of the third horizon
- Encouragement for pioneers
- A realistic view of the policy landscape (embrace H1 *and* H3)
- Evaluation based on third horizon intentions
- Funding transformative innovation

A Compelling Vision of the Third Horizon

As described earlier (see page 18), it is only the addition of a third horizon perspective that gets us out of a paradigm in which all innovation either improves or 'disrupts' the status quo. Envisioning a third horizon, fundamentally different from the first, opens up a space in which to design a longer-term transition from one dominant pattern of activity to another. It also sharpens our attention in the present so we notice instances where this new, transformed culture is already in evidence in some places and at some scale.

It is not unusual to find this vision already in place in government policy statements. The landscape is littered with aspirational visions for a better world, usually a decade or more away. What they tend to lack is any explicit acknowledgement that to achieve their goals will require a radical transformation in existing patterns and culture.

They can easily be interpreted – and usually are – as a call for an adjustment and rebalance in existing provision rather than a wholesale shift to a new viable pattern. Without an explicit third horizon policy goal, all systems and resources will inevitably be skewed towards maintaining and improving the status quo.

Thus it is a fundamental responsibility of government in particular to keep the strategic conversation about an H3 vision alive and dynamic in an ever-changing environment. Without this, strong natural forces of attraction will configure all innovation around existing rules, systems and infrastructure. Simply introducing the dynamics of the market into this space – competition, disruption, dedicated innovation funds – cannot change this dominant pattern.

It is the responsibility of those working at the strategic or policy-making level within the system to be aware of this dynamic. They need to be planning always both to keep the plane in the air and redesign it. They need to be adept at playing in both the first and the third horizon at the same time and conscious of the subtle, systems-level appreciation needed to enable a long-term transition from one to the other.

Encouragement for Pioneers

The Three Horizons framework describes and invites a journey from small beginnings to the ultimate realisation of a new culture. Those ready to set out on such a journey, to make a stand for and embody in the present a new way of doing things, however counter-cultural they may appear at the time, are our pioneers.

The problem for those in strategy and policy-making positions in systems and organisations is what stance to adopt towards these apparent mavericks and misfits. We know that amongst their projects are the seeds of future viability. We understand the need for all three roles – 'pioneers, settlers and town planners' – as agents of effective systems change. And we know the quote often attributed to Gandhi about how agents of culture change are often underestimated when they appear: "First they ignore you, then they laugh at you, then they fight you, then you win".

The difficulty is in knowing which of those pioneers always appearing on the fringes of any system are deserving of support – and then how to give that support. If a clear vision of a third horizon is articulated at the policy and strategy level then this is relatively straightforward.

First, the nature of the support need only take the form of permission to proceed, either explicit or implicit. Status quo, business-as-usual systems, institutions and assumptions will naturally hold back, rein in, capture, co-opt or fatally frustrate pioneering innovation that might otherwise have pointed to a different future. So the first requirement of policy and strategy is to acknowledge explicitly the need for more radical, pioneering innovation, which will inevitably appear counter-cultural. That gives permission to the pioneers. At the outset the role of first horizon authority is simply not to say "no".

Second, managerial policy-makers will worry that encouraging the visionaries will fragment and diversify what are generally intended to be universal systems. Hence "if we cannot do it for everyone, we should not do it for anyone". That is an entrenched mindset at odds with the dynamism demanded by the modern world. To overcome it, policy will need to become much more sophisticated about how it learns from experiment, how it extracts principles from one place to apply in another and so on. Just as medicine needs to move beyond a monotheistic belief in Randomised Control Trials and effectiveness based on averages drawn from big numbers, so too should policy become more adept at dealing with the unique, the personal, the specific, the set of $n=1$.

Dilemma thinking (see page 52) is a particularly powerful tool for making this shift. As issues arise that look like choices between mutually exclusive goods – such as universality and diversity – policy needs to practise dilemma thinking in order to get the best of both worlds, encouraging generative resolution rather than simplistic choices or flawed compromise. The dilemma space is a space of innovation and creative resolution which will naturally generate scores of powerful ideas for unlocking diversity of provision within overall standards of universality. These are precisely the conditions that policy should be seeking to provide – conditions that unlock abundance, complexity and life.

Third, those in strategic and policy-making positions might give active encouragement to pioneering initiatives that are consistent with their own third horizon aspirations. That means initiatives that are evidently underpinned by a similar set of values or cultural ambitions. They should look particularly for such initiatives *within* existing structures, because they particularly carry the promise of wider system transformation. They will always be there, but are not nearly as visible as start-ups outside the system.

The nature of the 'encouragement' in the early pioneering stage need be no more than appreciative attention: "We've seen what you're doing. It looks interesting. Carry on." But in order for a transformative initiative to complete the transition to a new 'patterned integrity' there will come a time when, having started by not saying "no", systems of first horizon authority actively have to say "yes".

A Realistic View of the Policy Landscape

One of the keys to transformative innovation's growth is that it needs to be consciously pursued within an evolving understanding of its surrounding institutional and policy context. At times that context can be frustrating. At other times it can serve as a source of support and useful elements of resourcing and infrastructure.

Such initiatives are always working with as smart an understanding of the surrounding landscape as possible, in full knowledge of the power of sunk cost infrastructure to constrain innovation. As one senior participant offering H1 support put it in a workshop for the SHINE project: "be aware that we have a black belt in taking promising organic initiatives and strangling the life out of them". This was Christensen's point about disruptive innovation. It is killed or ignored by managers not because they are doing a bad job, but precisely because they are performing their first horizon managerial role to perfection.

The equivalent in policy terms is to be found in Albert Hirschman's book *The Rhetoric of Reaction: perversity, futility, jeopardy*. His researches reveal three dominant patterns of H1 argument against progressive innovation: *perversity* (it will have perverse effects beyond those intended), *futility* (it will have no effect) and *jeopardy* (it might work but it puts previous success at risk). Both authors tap into a central truth of sound management: if there is tension between the new and the old, the radically different and the known, it must privilege the latter.

For the innovator, the challenge is not just to innovate but to do so in such a way that longer-term evolution of the system results – i.e. introducing the new in ways that allow it to flourish *in the presence of the old*. Policy and strategy must likewise acknowledge the tensions and dilemmas of change, where both the existing system and the imagined future have merit and value. It must be ready to free up some of the intellectual, physical and eventually financial resource currently locked in to the maintenance and improvement of the existing system – freeing it up to support H2 innovation with H3 aspirations and seeding creative resolution of the dilemmas even while the bulk of funding goes towards 'keeping the lights on'. The next chapter offers some thoughts on the institutional architecture that might support a dedicated innovation system for this purpose.

Evaluation Based on Third Horizon Intentions

Evaluation is always going to be a problem for any innovation with transformative intent. It needs to usher in a new culture whilst accounting for its performance in terms of existing (H1) priorities and assumptions.

More challenging still is the acknowledged difficulty of developing meaningful performance measures for an expanded worldview in which we are able to recognise that some results are realised on the inside, in the participants, and that many exist only in the relationships between them. The famous Peckham experiment in how to promote health in the 1930s found that no individual can be healthy alone. Health, as we noted at the outset, is a quality of life held in common. Love is another such quality. Language another.

A recent extensive evaluation report on the introduction of the Venezuelan El Sistema programme of classical music lessons for young people in deprived areas of Scotland (called 'Big Noise') found itself grappling with the same challenge. The evaluation – by Glasgow Centre for Population Health and others – discovered that it is the pattern of strong relationships formed through the programme that provides the active and transformative ingredient: "Big Noise musicians provide children with a trusted adult who recognises their strengths and achievements, provides praise and support, is a positive role model, and offers a consistent, secure and stable relationship. Musicians and volunteers are perceived as 'kind', 'nice', 'warm and friendly' and potential confidants... of particular benefit for children who have few (or no) other relationships of this sort."

The report then acknowledges a gaping hole where the capacity to recognise, measure or support this critical aspect of the project's effectiveness should be in terms of policy, strategy and evaluation: "People change lives, not services or programmes or music. At a societal level a challenging set of questions remain as to how this quality of relationship is conceptualised within policy, is represented and prioritised within funding criteria and structures and is planned for and implemented locally. And how can the quality of a relationship be satisfactorily measured or evaluated – and is this needed?"

This is a challenge that clearly needs to be addressed. It is up to the transformative innovators and their colleagues in policy and strategy to address it together. The first step is to acknowledge the difficulty. Transformative innovation cannot be evaluated simply according to the standards and processes of the first horizon. But it must be evaluated – not only to encourage the innovators, but to retain credibility within H1 power structures. As Jim Collins says in his *Good to Great and the Social Sectors: why business thinking is not the answer*, anyone who says that their version of success cannot be measured is guilty of intellectual laziness. One of the benefits of the Implemento tool described in the previous chapter is that it generates a coherent set of measures for the progress of an initiative, almost as a by-product of another conversation.

An essential element of the practical transition towards an H3 vision should be a disciplined approach to self-evaluation which recognises the value of experience and narrative alongside more conventional data.

The first requirement is to record the details of the journey. The native Alaskan healthcare service at South Central Foundation, the Nuka system of care, has been lauded across the world for its remarkable H1 performance measures. Those measures have resulted from a transformation in approach that has taken nearly 20 years to establish. Yet now the leaders of the approach can tell a powerful story – since they have submitted themselves to the most rigorous measurement and evaluation all along without becoming trapped by it (they say that a model is a shadow of reality, and that data based on any model is therefore a shadow of a shadow of reality).

Transformative innovation should certainly measure indicators that matter to existing systems. But at the same time those responsible for strategy and policy within those existing systems need somehow to acknowledge that the true value of such innovation a) will not be realised immediately b) is unlikely to progress in a linear and incremental fashion c) will generate results that may not be amenable to measurement based on rationalist, Enlightenment understandings and d) can only be meaningfully understood in the context of the third horizon vision it is designed to serve.

Hence the challenge for government and its agencies: to be ready to expand their own ways of knowing, to develop an appreciation of the dynamics of transition, and remain alive to 'results' in two cultures at the same time.

Financing Transformative Innovation

Financing transformative innovation raises some of the same issues addressed above in relation to evaluating it. So long as simple financial cost/benefit is the sole criterion for investment and funding decisions, the range of innovations on offer is likely to be skewed towards those that can deliver rapid efficiency savings in the existing system over those with longer-term transformative potential.

This is not necessarily a problem initially since it is a characteristic of transformative innovation that it is not very expensive. The resources it draws on to get started lie more in the domain of personal commitment. They are not financial. Margaret Hannah in her book *Humanising Healthcare* asks for an investment of just 1% of 1% of the annual healthcare budget in transformative innovation over ten years to shift most advanced healthcare systems to a new pattern of long-term viability.

This feels right: the initial financial investment required will be marginal. Yet at some point promising initiatives require the funding that will allow them to draw clear of the gravitational pull of improving 'business as usual'. That funding is usually very difficult to find from sources unfamiliar with transformative innovation and its special characteristics.

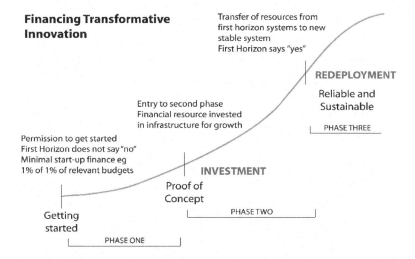

Financing Transformative Innovation

Transfer of resources from first horizon systems to new stable system
First Horizon says "yes"

REDEPLOYMENT

Reliable and Sustainable

PHASE THREE

Entry to second phase
Financial resource invested in infrastructure for growth

Permission to get started
First Horizon does not say "no"
Minimal start-up finance eg 1% of 1% of relevant budgets

INVESTMENT

Proof of Concept

PHASE TWO

Getting started

PHASE ONE

Typically such a project might be funded as an innovation for one year, take two years to achieve proof of concept and will only start to make a significant impact after three – just as in the SHINE case. For all the contemporary interest in social innovation 'labs', the fact is that no social innovation can be invented in the laboratory – it has to be developed in the real world. That takes time. Yet this period when the intervention is effectively being *invented* is judged by the standards of a fully functional product (an innovation).

IFF's experience suggests that a number of factors need to be borne in mind by funders, whether government or philanthropic, seeking to sponsor truly transformative innovation.

The first is to allow more time for radical innovation to prove itself. More and more funds are moving in the opposite direction – small-scale, rapid returns – in order to encourage more small tests of change and find out quickly which to scale and which to abandon, preferably within a single financial year.

That is fine for technical improvements, but culture shift takes longer. The SHINE project team working on a transformative innovation in older people's care knew this and bent the funding rules from the outset to give themselves a more realistic timescale. Bidding for a one-year 'invest to save' grant, they asked for the one-year funding, offered milestones for gauging progress at the end of year one but proposed a return on the investment only at the end of year two. It is to the great credit of the Health Foundation that they agreed the grant on that basis.

This suggests an innovation in how to think about grant-making and other forms of investment in innovation. Funders need to think both about the quantity of the initial investment *and* a reasonable break-even time for the kinds of projects they wish to support. Transformative innovation is likely to take longer to prove its effectiveness, precisely because it is working against the grain of business-as-usual systems.

The application form for transformative innovation funds might therefore include milestones to plot progress and a longer break-even time. The form could also be framed around the three horizons, asking those bidding to demonstrate a) their desired third horizon, reassuring funders that they genuinely have a transformative intent; b) their understanding of the H1 drivers in the system that they will need to contend with in order to stay true to that intent; and c) the kinds of measures the project itself will generate intrinsically to demonstrate to its leaders that it is on track to fulfil the transformative ambition (evaluation from an H3 perspective).

A second feature of these kinds of initiative is that the funding needs tend to change over time. In the early phase it is a characteristic of transformative innovation that it does not require much money. Indeed, if innovation can only be stimulated by the provision of a specific innovation fund it is a fairly good rule of thumb that it will not be transformative.

But there does come a point where funding *is* required. It usually occurs a little way into a project, after two or three years, the time it takes for a shift in practice, in people, in culture to start to make a difference. Funding is generally difficult to find at that point. Innovation funds are no longer interested since the idea is not new. Regular mainstream funding is not yet available since the innovation has yet to make a significant impact on H1 targets so the transfer of resources from existing to emergent systems is not yet justified.

Hence there is a specific gap in the funding ecosystem for what we might call 'second phase transformative innovation'. IFF is establishing a dedicated Transformative Innovation Fund for precisely this purpose. Other funders and organisations should do likewise. The criteria should be easy to fashion from the understanding of transformative innovation offered in this book. The three suggestions offered on the previous page for inclusion in any application for funding would be a good start.

Project leaders themselves will know when this 'second phase' moment is likely to arrive. They should be able to articulate at that time the case for the timely cash injection that will allow a promising experiment to establish itself as a significant new pattern even within the limiting patterns and assumptions of the first horizon. This is the entrepreneurial moment when we move from the struggles of invention to the disciplined processes of innovation and improvement – the moment of truth.

The final phase of a successful transformative innovation is the shift from one infrastructure to another. This is the point where resources that have been sunk into the fixed infrastructure of the first horizon can be freed up and redeployed by investing in the structures configuring the new patterned integrity of the third horizon.

A funding system based on a strategic understanding of this transition will think at this stage less in terms of 'invest to save' and more in terms of 'redeployment' of existing resources. This is not an investment strategy predicated on cost savings but on redeploying resources in new ways to realise an aspirational new pattern of activity. The native Alaskan healthcare system, for example, has not resulted in huge cost savings. But it has avoided the exponential cost *rises* that are endemic in other advanced healthcare systems, and is delivering outcomes and quality that those other systems can only dream of.

In sum, the purpose, progress and profile of transformative innovation is distinctive and requires a distinctive approach to funding to match. Simply acknowledging this is a good starting point for policy and strategy. Setting aside a marginal proportion of any innovation funding specifically for transformative innovation is a simple way to begin experimenting with the practical details of such an approach and could itself be a potentially culture-changing innovation.

Further Reading – details at www.iffpraxis.com/ti

Humanising Healthcare: patterns of hope for a system under strain (especially chapter 6 on Randomised Controlled Trials as 'a self-limiting improvement methodology' and chapter 8 on Designing for Transition)

Everything Flows

'Everything flows'. Heraclitus's observation was quoted in Chapter 2. It is fundamental to the practice of transformative innovation. It reminds us that every stable structure can also be seen as a slowly evolving process, held in place by a complex and dynamic pattern of activities that is always in flux.

We live in a world always in motion, in which patterns of relationship and activity are growing, developing, struggling and declining all the time in each other's contexts. These are natural processes, the processes of life itself.

The traditional Western view of how to take effective action in these circumstances is familiar. We set our goal, plan our route, marshal our resources and execute the journey from A to B. We impose ourselves on the world to create something we call 'change.' The fact that as we do so everything around us changes at the same time is an awkward reality, usually dismissed with the phrase 'unintended consequences'.

The Eastern view, eloquently expressed in Sun Tzu's *The Art of War*, is very different. The highest triumph of strategy in this view is to 'win the war without fighting.' This approach sees the landscape as being in a state of continuous change, much of it at a scale or a pace or a subtlety that escapes our attention. François Jullien talks about the 'potentialities' in the landscape in his book *A Treatise on Efficacy: between Western and Chinese thinking*, perhaps the best modern exposition of this way of thinking.

On this view, we do not bring about the change we desire by imposing our goals on the external world. Instead we read the landscape with such exquisite discernment that we see better than others the possibilities it might offer and act in tune with them to bring them into being. We win the battle without fighting not by seeking to impose change, but by placing ourselves in the landscape with a deeper awareness of the present and a greater strategic vision of its potential than our opponent, who ends up in a dead end, cornered, on the low ground, disadvantaged – and surrenders.

The Three Horizons framework (along with much else in this book) encourages this more dynamic and systemic appreciation of the landscape. It invites us to practise 'holism with focus', to see beyond the systems and structures of immediate concern to us to the dynamic patterns of activity that maintain them. It highlights our own role in sustaining the apparently stable patterns of the first horizon through our participation: every time we use the railways, shop at a supermarket, drive to work, take our children to school, we are helping to maintain these social structures and the diverse pattern of allied activities that sustain them in an overall pattern of life.

If we look deeper we can see those aspects of the current pattern that are intentionally maintained and those that are not. Many of our complex, messy, systemic challenges arise precisely because they lie outside the intent of those who built the first horizon patterns that now dominate. Like obesity or climate change, they are unintended consequences, the effect of a complex interaction between many different aspects of our current way of life.

Patterns of Renewal

Nothing lasts forever. There are dynamics already in play that are undermining the effectiveness of all first horizon systems. These too shall pass. The question therefore is not *whether* a transition to a new pattern will occur, but how and when. And the answer will depend on how well we have organised our society to support the process of renewal.

In *Three Horizons* Bill Sharpe describes two areas in which we have intentionally designed patterns of renewal at a societal level to enable natural processes of dynamism and change:

> *In democracies we have invented a social system that generally is able to accommodate change without the need for collapse and renewal of the system of governance itself. In earlier times, and still in other parts of the world, we are familiar with societal change requiring civil war, revolution, collapse or some other discontinuous change in the institutions of governance themselves. Democracies do not work because we all agree on everything, but because the process of disagreement is structured and resolves itself in agreed ways. To champion change in a democracy you set out your manifesto and campaign for election. Your manifesto may include changes to the constitution that governs the democracy itself.*
>
> *Another example is the way we manage our economic life. We have found out the hard way that planned economies don't work very well, partly because they are very poor at adapting to change.*

Their suppression of variety in the name of efficiency prevents the processes of change introducing and scaling up new things through the messy competitive processes of innovation. Market economies are set up in ways that specifically support continuous change. Established H1 companies extend their familiar products and services as far as they can, sometimes absorbing H2 innovations, but over time most of them will be displaced by new players with accompanying waves of creative destruction across whole industries – most companies do not last more than fifty years as leaders in their industries, or even as independent companies at all.

We find no such intentionally structured patterns of renewal in the social and public spheres that this book addresses. The natural process in which one dominant pattern of life gives way more or less gracefully over time to another better suited to the emerging landscape remains haphazard, uncoordinated and lacking in structure in these fields.

There are countless actors and agencies taking on the transitional work John Vasconcellos describes: hospice work for the dying culture and midwifery for the new. But they are for the most part working against the grain of dominant first horizon structures and systems which crush the life from the natural processes of renewal on which they rely.

The previous chapter addressed how policy, strategy and finance can adapt to serve these processes of renewal. This final chapter offers some first thoughts on the structures and institutions we may need to develop to embed such processes. What might a dedicated infrastructure of support for transformative innovation look like?

Cultural Renewal

One clue lies in IFF's study of Watershed, the cultural cinema and digital creativity hub in Bristol already mentioned in Chapter 4.

When we became involved in 2008, Bristol already had a growing reputation for its culture of innovation, particularly in the creative industries. The World Economic Forum had just identified it as one of 100 creative environments around the world combining innovation talent, a culture of collaboration and a willingness to source ideas outside traditional boundaries. It was identified as a "hotspring of innovation".

There was a strong intuition that Watershed itself was making a critical contribution to this success story, but nobody could quite figure out how. The UK Creative Economy Programme had a go: "Watershed is a prime example of a highly connected, flexible, porous piece of cultural and creative infrastructure, of which there are too few examples. Watershed is more than just an arts cinema. It is at once a cultural centre, a business broker, a social networker, a research and innovation facility, a café/bar and a cultural tourist attraction".

This is no more than a description, albeit a beguiling one. What it is pointing to however, in our terms, is the possibility that Watershed is indeed 'a highly connected, flexible, porous piece of cultural and creative infrastructure', that is intentionally designed to facilitate the natural processes of cultural growth and renewal in the city.

Our subsequent investigation, working closely with Watershed over a couple of years, discovered that the organisation embodies many of the capacities for transformative innovation outlined in previous chapters. Indeed, the report *Producing the Future: Understanding Watershed's Role in Ecosystems of Cultural Innovation* can be read as the organisational equivalent of *SHINE: Changing the Culture of Care*. The latter is a detailed case study of a particular transformative initiative (see page 21), whilst the

Watershed study explores the process of developing a dedicated infrastructure to support such innovation across the system.

Looking at Watershed through a Three Horizons lens identifies how it acts as an innovation system in the second horizon space. It takes creative complexity and helps to shape it into viable patterns of activity that can sustain themselves in the dominant culture and in so doing advance cultural change: in other words, the practice of transformative innovation.

In the world of the arts we can frequently see isolated, novel, visionary acts of artistic invention that break from established patterns and form an initial 'creative integrity', the third horizon in the present. These are taking place all the time.

The move from 'creative integrity' to 'patterned integrity' occurs as these one-off acts are brought into relationship, creating new patterns of shared meaning, new cultural genres. Watershed was active, for example, in the early days of 'monumental media' (projecting images on to buildings) and of 'street gaming' (mobile technology enabling virtual reality games in real streets) – both now familiar genres. If this move to 'genre', a new established pattern in its own right, sounds arcane, notice that we now capture the same shift in everyday language when people start to notice a novel practice repeating and ask: 'is that now a thing?'

Part of Watershed's skill in this process comes through artful navigating of the dilemmas of the second horizon. The core dilemma often lies between the economy of money and the economy of meaning. Watershed operates in the space of creative resolution of these two patterns of value: steering between the extremes of intensely meaningful work that nobody wants and highly profitable work that fails to enrich the meaning of our lives.

Discovering, exploring, creating and strengthening new patterns of activity, consciously navigating the value tensions in play between the old and the new and between different actors in the system, is what Watershed is so good at. It is an example of the organisation as producer.

This is a vital role in feeding the processes of renewal. In the previous example of democracy we might see political parties as playing a producer role – bringing policy preferences and people together and exercising judgement about which pattern is most likely to generate a stable constituency of support. Likewise in the economy, venture capitalists take a position by bringing resources together with creative business ideas and use their own judgement to grow the company.

One of the conclusions of our work together with Watershed was that they needed to 'grow more producers' (which they have done – and gone from strength to strength). It is one of the few places I know that actively and explicitly develops producer competencies.

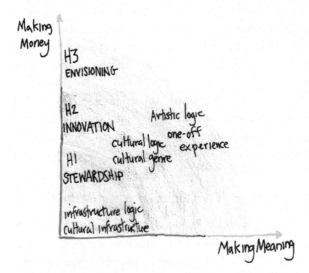

What we might conclude from this story, echoing the UK Creative Economy Programme, is that there are indeed too few examples of this kind of 'highly connected, flexible, porous piece of cultural and creative infrastructure'. We certainly need more in the big fields of social and public policy – health, social care, education, prisons, community development, inequalities and so on.

At least the idea of infrastructure for innovation systems is beginning to gain traction. In 2015, for example, the Joseph Rowntree Charitable Trust and the Friends Provident Foundation chose to invest £250,000 over three years in the Finance Innovation Lab to establish 'an infrastructure for systems change' in the financial system.

Likewise, the Ford Foundation has decided to place more emphasis on institutions alongside its traditional commitment to ideas and individuals. As their President, Darren Walker, puts it: "building durable institutions and networks will be among our highest priorities because, as we've seen throughout our history, they represent the infrastructure on which movements for change are built. Institutions are hubs for gathering and aggregating talent; they provide the platforms that help accelerate and sustain social change."

Perhaps we are beginning to see a natural move towards investment in infrastructure intentionally designed to support processes of social and cultural change and the 'creative advance into novelty'.

Infrastructure for Transformative Innovation

Whilst the Watershed experience is encouraging, even in the world of the arts it remains an exception and little understood. Mainstream appreciation of how to support innovation, even in the public, cultural and social sectors, is still mostly based on private sector practice. Yet this can be misleading and risks embedding systems in the public and social spheres that will favour incremental improvement over radical transformation. Innovation starts with good ideas. The challenge of coming up with them is common to all sectors. But once it has a good idea, the private sector can pretty much rely on the market to do the rest. There are natural patterns of renewal.

The critical challenge, as Geoffrey Moore put it, is "crossing the chasm" between the early adopters and the early majority, the visionaries who will take up a new practice and the pragmatists who are needed to make it sustainable. Early adopters like to try new things. The early majority are more wary. They will only take something up if they know it works better than what they have already. Once the pragmatists have adopted something, sales scale naturally and, as an entrepreneur, you start to make money – which is the object of the exercise.

This is the natural order of things in Silicon Valley, for example. Tech guru David Weekly suggests that the place works because nobody tries to make it work. Start-ups release ideas into the market, governments don't pick winners, investors follow the money. As Weekly puts it: "Silicon Valley's startups are stupid, its government is stupid, and its investors are stupid. Companies are successful here because business intelligence is distributed, and the ultimate arbiter of correctness is the market."

It really is that simple. 'Stupid' in this context is good. The lack of any preferred direction is fine and essential to the effective functioning of the renewal process. But in other spheres of life we suffer the consequences of this stupidity – we get left with 'unintended' results like climate change and obesity. As we have seen many times in this book, the patterns of renewal that have shaped the market will not deliver transformative innovation in the public and social sectors.

The previous chapter offered some thoughts on how policy, strategy and finance can adapt to enable transformative innovation, to recognise it as distinctive and support it accordingly.

At the level of intermediary infrastructure, the experience of Watershed is encouraging. So too are the first stirrings of interest in supporting organisations, institutions and ecosystems to provide stable systems of innovation outside the commercial sphere.

That leaves the level of practice. The traditional top-down way to support innovation in times of big systems change is to provide instructions and guidance to would-be innovators – and then to inspect for achievement and share 'best practice'. Transformative innovation cannot be pursued in this way and will either be ignored or misrepresented in the search for 'best practice'.

The evidence of the SHINE project, amongst others, suggests that what practitioners actually need are processes, materials, prompts, advice, experience and company to help them think through their next moves, their change initiatives, for themselves.

That is the main reason why this book has been written. But it also acts as a gateway to a wider set of resources in a dedicated Practice Centre at www.iffpraxis.com. This includes:

- simple tools and processes such as those outlined in previous chapters to help individuals and teams develop and pursue transformative proposals.

- transition tools to keep the process on track over time.

- resources for the producer competencies and for peer support that help with the human aspects of change.

- a scanning function to highlight examples of inspiring practice in the present that suggest a third horizon vision is indeed achievable.

- a dedicated Transformative Innovation Fund to invest in such innovation at the point where initial funding has expired even as the innovation is finally starting to gain traction.

As has been stressed many times throughout this book, transformative innovation is a social process, a process of social learning pursued in a human system. Hence the rule: no solo climbers. We need peer support, company on the journey. Equally, these materials and other resources will come to life only through shared experience and in community.

Part of the infrastructure of support therefore must also involve configuring the community of transformative innovators, a community of purpose with its eyes on aspirational change. And lying behind this community is another – of experienced practitioners, capable trainers and mentors, sources of guidance and advice including members of IFF's international clan.

The infrastructure IFF is putting in place is very much a private initiative, albeit based on substantial international support and experience. It is itself a transformative innovation, the attempt to establish a new pattern – a pattern that can be realised at any level from local to global.

We hope that in time every 21st century government, every significant governmental agency, every funder or promoter of social change will develop its own systems along these lines. Over time we will together establish in the landscape the patterns of renewal that we need if we are to encourage and support transformative change.

The Permission Slip

With these systems of support and renewal in place it will be 'safe' to introduce one final piece of infrastructure which should have the effect of opening all systems up to transformative innovation. This is the permission slip.

I came across it first in Washington in the days of Vice President Al Gore's reinventing government programme in the early 1990s. It was issued to all federal government employees and was printed on a business card. On one side was a statement from the Vice President: "You have the authority and the responsibility to make government work better and cost less". On the other side was an injunction to ask yourself five questions:

1. Is it good for my customers?

2. Is it legal and ethical?

3. Is it something I am willing to be accountable for?

4. Is it consistent with my agency's mission?

5. Am I using my time wisely?

It then concluded, over Al Gore's signature, "Is the answer yes to all these questions? If so you don't need permission, you already have it. JUST DO IT!"

This is a wonderfully simple intervention. It has the potential to release the creativity in the system. It is a classic piece of 'social acupuncture' as described in Chapter 3. I have tried to introduce it since then in all kinds of different government and social sector contexts, but always without success. The challenge has always been to identify the constraints for any particular policy area or system or agency which need to be implied in the questions.

I understand this caution. As it stands, this simple card might be read as an invitation to chaos. The questions, the reference to the "agency's mission" and the assumption that everyone will know and agree on what working "better" will look like might not provide enough structure to reassure first horizon managers that all will be well and failures will not be significant. With no natural patterns of renewal in the public and social sectors we are rightly cautious of a policy that simply invites a thousand flowers to bloom.

Those patterns of renewal can now be put in place. The practical guidance in this book should be enough to reassure system leaders that they can fashion policy, strategy and finance to encourage the transition from a failing system towards a new third horizon vision. There is a sound body of knowledge, based on experience, about how to navigate that transition in practice, starting with small steps and drawing on resources of personal commitment and imagination. The supportive infrastructure needed to give those initiatives the best chance of success is available at some scale, and sound design principles are available for others to provide more.

All of these moves help to take the 'risk' out of opening up our systems to the transformative impulse that lies within them – just as it lies in all of us. Given that the explicit role of first horizon systems in the early stages of transformative innovation is to give permission, to 'not say no', it would be a smart piece of enabling policy to introduce a version of this card as a signal of intent and an invitation to everyone to participate in renewing the system.

If you have read this far you will know you don't actually need permission to get started. Indeed, most readers will have picked up this guide precisely because they recognise they are pioneering transformative innovation already. But it always helps to reflect on one's practice, to learn from others and to know that there are systems of support available should we need them.

With the IFF Practice Centre in place and the experience of the extended IFF community behind it we are now issuing our own permission slip. To recall the description of transformative innovation at the very start of this guide, it gives permission "to act in tune with and realise our deeper aspirations in a complex world rather than just settle for fixing what's failing."

Just do it.

Transformative Innovation Permission Slip

You have the authority and responsibility to help shift your system towards an aspirational third horizon vision of the future.

Ask yourself:

1. Is it good for the people I serve and care about?
2. Is it legal, ethical and in tune with my professional values?
3. Am I willing to take responsibility and be accountable for it?
4. Can I find a friend willing to join me?
5. Does it embody the third horizon in the present?
6. Can I get started with little or no additional finance?
7. Is the answer 'yes' to all these questions?

If so, don't ask for permission - you already have it. Just do it!

IFF's international clan is a diverse group of individuals with different perspectives, disciplines, expertise, life experience and so on. They all share a commitment to IFF's work and to supporting each other as fellow members of a rich learning community. (Note: * denotes Founding Fellow)

Martin Albrow * Fellow of the Käte Hamburger Kolleg, Bonn University; author of *The Global Age: state and society beyond modernity.*

Ruth Anderson * Chief Executive, Barataria Foundation, Scotland.

Tony Beesley * Conceptual artist and cartoonist.

Max Boisot * Professor at ESADE, University of Ramon Llull in Barcelona; Associate Fellow at the Said Business School, University of Oxford. Author of *Knowledge Assets: securing competitive advantage in the information economy.* (died 2011)

Roberto Carneiro * Former Education Minister; President of Grupo Forum, Portugal; UNESCO International Commission on Education for the 21st Century.

Napier Collyns * Co-founder, Global Business Network (GBN), San Francisco, USA.

Thomas Corver Corver Management Consultancy; former strategy coordinator at ING bank, The Netherlands.

Frank Crawford Educator; former HM Chief Inspector of Schools in Scotland.

Pamela Deans * IFF recorder; ForthRoad Limited, Scotland.

Roanne Dods	Former Director, Jerwood Charitable Foundation.
Kate Ettinger	Senior Fellow, Center for Health Professions, UCSF; Health Care Ethics Consultant-Mediator & Social Change Architect, San Francisco, USA.
Jim Ewing	Designer of practical strategies & methods for sustained transformational achievement. Author of *TransforMAP* and *Council*, conceptware and software for organisational development. Seattle, USA. (died 2014)
Brian Goodwin *	Schumacher College, Devon and Santa Fe Institute; author of *How the Leopard Changed Its Spots: the evolution of complexity*. (died 2009)
Bo Gyllenpalm	President SITSERV AB, Sweden; faculty member Fielding Graduate University, USA.
Timo Hämäläinen	Strategic Research Fellow, Finnish Innovation Fund, Sitra, Helsinki.
Mike Hambly *	Former Director, Scottish Enterprise; Chief Executive, Digital Animations Group, Glasgow.
Phil Hanlon	Professor of Public Health, University of Glasgow (retired).
Margaret Hannah	Director of Public Health, NHS Fife.
Pat Heneghan *	Director, ForthRoad Limited, Scotland.
David Hodgson	Co-founder, The Idea Hive and Connective, San Francisco, USA.
Rebecca Hodgson *	Researcher, IFF.

Tony Hodgson *	Director, Decision Integrity Ltd; World Modelling Research, IFF; Founder, H3Uni; author of *Ready for Anything*.
Robert Horn	Visiting Scholar in the Human Sciences and Technology Advanced Research Institute (H-STAR) at Stanford University and CEO, MacroVU Inc.
Kees van der Heijden *	Professor at Templeton College, Oxford; author of *Scenarios: the art of strategic conversation*.
Ken Ideus	Principal, I-Deos Consulting and Express Yourself; Chancellor & Co-founder, Mikesi University, South Sudan.
Adam Kahane	Reos Partners and University of Oxford, author of *Solving Tough Problems*, *Power and Love* and *Transformative Scenario Planning*.
Pat Kane *	Writer, theorist and musician, Glasgow; author of *The Play Ethic*.
Eamonn Kelly *	Chief Marketing Officer for Strategy and Operations, Deloitte; author of *Powerful Times: rising to the challenge of our uncertain world*.
Rajiv Kumar	Senior Fellow, Centre for Policy Research India; former Director General, Federation of Indian Chambers of Commerce and Industry.
Graham Leicester *	Director, IFF; co-author of *Dancing at the Edge: culture, competence and organisation in the 21st century*.
Alison Linyard	Producer, NHS Fife and Glasgow Centre for Population Health, partnership working and person-centred practice.
David Lorimer *	Programme Director, Scientific & Medical Network.

Charles Lowe *	Consultant, Former head of e-government BT.
Wendy Luhabe *	Bridging the Gap, South Africa; author of *Defining Moments: experiences of black executives in South Africa's workplace.*
Andrew Lyon *	Converger (retired), IFF.
Harry MacMillan *	Former Chair of IFF Trustees; Vice-President for Public Affairs in Scotland, BP.
James McCormick	Scotland Adviser, Joseph Rowntree Foundation.
Arun Maira *	Former member, Planning Commission, Govt. of India; author of *Redesigning the Aeroplane While Flying: reforming institutions.*
Wolfgang Michalski *	WM International; formerly Chief Advisor to the Secretary-General of the OECD; author of *Capitalising on Change in a Globalising World.*
Maureen O'Hara *	Chair of the Psychology Department, National University, La Jolla, CA; President Emerita, Saybrook Graduate School, San Francisco; co-author of *Dancing at the Edge: culture, competence and organisation in the 21st century.*
Aftab Omer	President, Meridian University, California.
Ian Page *	Former Research Manager/Futurist, HP Corporate Labs.
David Peat	Theoretical physicist; Director of the Pari Center for New Learning, Tuscany, Italy.
Maria Pereira	Clinton Climate Initiative; former investment manager; author of *A Banker Reflects on Money, Love and Virtue.*

Noah Raford	Adviser, Special Projects, Office of the Prime Minister, UAE.
Nick Rengger *	Professor of Political Theory and International Relations, University of St Andrews; author *International Relations, Political Theory and the Problem of Order*.
Vineeta Shanker	Independent researcher on faiths in the global economy; previously project director, World Faiths Development Dialogue.
Bill Sharpe	Independent researcher in science, technology and society; Visiting Professor, University of the West of England; author of *Economies of Life* and *Three Horizons: the patterning of hope*.
Denis Stewart	Converger, IFF Ireland; formerly, roving educator.
Daniel Wahl	Transition Catalyst & Resilience Research, IFF (Spain, Germany, UK); former Director of Findhorn College.
Jennifer Williams	Artist; former Director, Centre for Creative Communities, UK.
Mark Woodhouse *	Professor of Philosophy Emeritus at Georgia State University, USA; author of *Paradigm Wars: worldviews for a new age*.
Chris Yapp	Specialist in technology, policy and innovation and Senior Associate Fellow at the Institute of Governance and Public Management, Warwick Business School.

About IFF

IFF (International Futures Forum) is a non-profit organisation established in 2001 to support a transformative response to complex and confounding challenges and to restore the capacity for effective action in today's powerful times.

At its heart is a deeply informed inter-disciplinary and international learning community of individuals from a range of backgrounds covering diverse perspectives, countries and disciplines. Over fifteen years this group has generated a series of powerful insights and concepts which have been progressively tested in practice with business, governments and communities.

This learning is brought together in the practice of transformative innovation. It is IFF's mission both to continue refining the practice in light of experience and to make the tools, processes, attitudes, frameworks and conceptual breakthroughs that support it as widely available as possible – fostering practical hope and wise initiative.

About the Author

Graham Leicester is a founder and Director of IFF. He previously ran Scotland's leading think tank, the Scottish Council Foundation, founded in 1997. From 1984 to1995 he served as a diplomat in HM Diplomatic Service, specialising in China (he speaks Mandarin Chinese) and the EU. Between 1995 and 1997 he was senior research fellow with the Constitution Unit at University College London.

He has also worked as a freelance professional cellist, including with the BBC Concert Orchestra. He has strong interests in governance, innovation, education and healthcare and has previously worked with OECD, the World Bank Institute and other agencies on the themes of governance in a knowledge society and the governance of the long term. He is the author, with Maureen O'Hara, of *Dancing at the Edge: competence, culture and organisation in the 21st century.*

www.iffpraxis.com

ABOUT THE PUBLISHER

Triarchy Press is an independent publisher of new alternative thinking (altThink) about organisations and society – and practical ways to apply that thinking. Where *Transformative Innovation* focuses on the infrastructure, strategies, practices and processes required to implement radical change in the non-commercial sectors, other authors focus more widely on social and cultural transformation, and on innovation in the commercial sector. Other Triarchy Press titles consider emergent changes in fields like walking, dance, performance and psychotherapy. All exemplify the kind of practical hope and wise initiative pioneered by IFF:

- IFF's books on designing resilience, humanising healthcare, transforming education, Three Horizons thinking and things to do in a conceptual emergency are all published by Triarchy.

- Planning for the future is also a highly technical matter and one long-established approach is Scenario Planning. *Facing the Fold* brings together a collection of the best essays on the subject by its leading proponent, James (Jay) Ogilvy.

- Stephen Millett's guide to forecasting and planning, *Managing the Future,* offers a straightforward approach to strategic planning in business. Alongside it, Tricia Lustig's *Strategic Foresight* presents tools for navigating into an uncertain future.

- Daniel Wahl's *Designing Regenerative Cultures* has been called "an extraordinary intellectual and analytical resource, providing as good a picture of contemporary holistic, systems-based thinking as you're likely to find" by Jonathon Porritt (former Director of Friends of the Earth and Chair of the UK's Ecology Party (now the Green Party).

www.triarchypress.net/the-future